ASTROLOGY

FROM A TO Z

Illustrated by
JILL KARLA SCHWARZ

By
ELEANOR BACH

ASTROLOGY
FROM

TO

An Illustrated Source Book

M. EVANS AND COMPANY, INC.
New York

Library of Congress Cataloging-in-Publication Data

Bach, Eleanor.
    Astrology from A to Z: an illustrated source book / by Eleanor Bach; illustrated
by Jill Karla Schwartz.
        p.   cm.
    Reprint. Originally published : New York : Philosophical Library, 1990.
    ISBN 0-87131-674-9
    1. Astrology—Dictionaries.   I. Title.
BF 1655.B33   1991
133.5'03—dc20   91-17601
                                                                                    CIP

1992 Edition

M. Evans and Company, Inc.
216 East 49th Street
New York, New York 10017
Manufactured in the United States of America
9 8 7 6 5 4 3 2 1

To our dear

Mother Earth

Note: Important terms and concepts in current usage will be in capital letters; others will be in lower-case, briefly defined and in some cases simply recorded without comment.

Abscission: Literally "cutting off." Also know as "frustration." A term solely applicable to horary questions. When a planet is moving into aspect with a second planet, and a third planet, either swifter or nearer, forms an aspect with the second planet before the initial aspect has been completed, the initial aspect and its potential effects are cut off or frustrated. (see Horary Astrology)

ACD: Adjusted Calculation Date. This is the date—the month and day of the year—that the noon or midnight positions of the planets in the ephemeris correspond to in the progressed horoscope. Due to the proliferation of computer programs that perform the calculation for finding this date instantly, the need to know the technique for its calculation is fast becoming unnecessary.

Affliction: A term used by medieval astrologers to describe harsh aspects between planets or unfortunate locations of planets. Forget it. No contemporary astrologer would be caught dead using this negative, discouraging, and inappropriate term, that is unless s/he insists upon living in the dark ages. There are a few of those.

AIR SIGNS: The Air Triplicity: Libra, Aquarius, and Gemini. One Cardinal, one Fixed, and one Mutable. They are also called the "sweet" signs. In astrology the Air signs represent the psychological function of thinking. The thinking function facilitates relationship because without thought it is impossible to look outside of self and understand another person, to deal objectively with a troubling conflict, to solve a problem through intelligent discernment, or to comprehend the meaning and significance of events. This ability to direct attention to "the other" is a very ingratiating quality which is why these signs are referred to as sweet. They are also called relationship signs because their zodiacal names of the signs, the symbolism of their glyphs, and the circumstances indicated by their corresponding houses all imply the involvement of one or more persons.

Alignments: Conjunctions or oppositions exact in both latitude and longitude; considered powerful aspects.

ALTITUDE: The distance of a star or planet from the horizon, measured at right angles to the plane of the horizon.

ANATOMY AND THE SIGNS: The signs have rulership over the different parts of the body. This can be quite astonishingly literal at times.

When one of the following signs is rising or is one in which the Sun, Moon, or an unusual concentration of planets is found, there will be an emphasis on the part of the body over which that sign has rulership. The Ascendant (or Rising Sign) in particular has great influence over bodily appearance, but in fact it is impossible to find a pure example of any sign. Everyone is a blend in varying degrees of several signs and the characteristics they decree.

Aries—The head, scull, and upper teeth. Often there is a scar on the head; a tendency to fall or get hit on the head. I have known a little Aries boy to butt into his mother with his head. Women will often do outrageous things with their hair, dying it pitch black, platinum blond, or red; frizzing it, curling it, or shaving it. Sometimes there is an emphasis on all of the paraphernalia of facial make-up: rouge, lipstick, mascara, eye shadow, etc. One often finds arched brows producing a haughty or surprised expression. This is the Easter sign, the sign of the Easter bonnet; hats have their heyday at this time of the year. Men are inclined to baldness.

Taurus—The throat, ears, Eustachian tubes, lower teeth, and cervical vertebrae. Often unusually long necks are found in this sign or, conversely, necks which are short and thick—in any case there is an emphasis on the neck. There is a tendency to sore throats. There are often metabolic problems, for the throat is the seat of the thyroid. Or there may be sugar problems. The voice box is in the throat, and one often finds operatic voices or a talent for singing and an especially keen sensitivity to sound.

Gemini—The lungs, arms and hands, clavicles, and upper dorsal nerves. Often there are respiratory problems, and in this sign of communication a tendency to talk with the hands, or to use the hands as an accompaniment to language. Linguists may have an emphasis of planets in this sign. Often there are skillful hands, and some natives are ambidextrous, or prestidigitators.

Cancer—The breasts and stomach. Both men and women often have a sort of skinny-legged, top-heavy appearance, especially if this sign is rising. Subject to stomach problems, ulcers. In this highly emotional sign, emotional nourishment is emphasized, nourishment on the infantile level. They may be bottle babies in more than one sense.

Leo—The heart and upper back. A regal sign, proud and dramatic. Unbending, inflexible. But pride goeth before a fall, and one wonders if heart attack is not precipitated by hurt feelings (the heart is a symbol for feeling), excessive hurt pride, or injuries to self-dignity. These people are often very broad-backed. Men tend to baldness, and women often comb their hair like lions' manes and have deep dramatic voices.

Virgo—The small intestine and the uterus or womb. Sensitive digestive system. The assimilative part of the body through which body building occurs, building into self. Body-building goes on in the womb, too. This is a laboring, productive sign. There is sometimes great beauty and delicacy of feature in this sign. Usually flat-backed with a lean backside.

Libra—The lower back, lumbar nerves, and kidneys. These natives often have a sort of swinging, bouncy step, and good balance. There may be a noticeable emphasis on "the buns," a backside that calls attention to itself. There is usually a very delicate bone structure, a chin that is not exactly receding but that is definitely not prominent; often an oval face.

Scorpio—The excretory system, including the large colon, anus, urethra in male and female, and in the male the penis, and scrotum. In the male, both urine and semen are discharged). Obviously with this emphasis there is a possibility of plumbing problems, in the body and yes, in the home. These natives are often extremely seductive and fascinatingly attractive. They project an intensity that can be irresistibly compelling.

Sagittarius—The hams and thighs, sciatic nerves, and the fleshy part of the body. Sagittarians tend to be big and to put on weight. They are often tall, long legged, and walk a lot. However, one occasionally comes across a diminutive Sagittarian who is big in feelings and enthusiasms if not physique, the exception that proves the rule. Often when they laugh or smile their eyes sort of get lost in narrowed slits.

Capricorn—The skin, bones, knees, and patella. The sign of sensitivity and depth; of structure and form. There may be skin problems or exceedingly beautiful skin. There may be problems with teeth, bones, and knees. Often there is an exceptional agility in climbing. These people usually age well, looking much younger than their years.

Aquarius—The lower limbs from knee to ankle, tibia, and blood. Often there are circulatory problems in this sign. Handsome features, cool, unruffled visage. Detached "above the battle" mien.

Pisces—The feet, from ankle downwards and the lymphatic system. There are lots of dancers in this sign for Pisces is very responsive to rhythmical flow. Or on the other hand, there may be foot problems. Often there is a heavy-lidded, sad looking expression about the eyes, with eyebrows that are circumflex, angling upwards on the inside, when Pisces is emphasized or rising.

ANGLES: This is a term used by astrologers to identify the extremely important great circles of reference that intersect the Ecliptic: the Horizon, linking the Ascendant-Descendant points of intersection and the Meridian, linking the Medium Coeli (Zenith)-Imum Coeli (Nadir) points of intersection. Their right angle relationship defines the Cardinal Cross which identifies the houses adjacent to these angles. (see House Categories)

ANGULAR HOUSES (see House Categories)

ANGULAR PLANETS: Nowadays planets are said to be angular if they are in the first, fourth, seventh, or tenth houses, or within five degrees of the cusp of the Ascendant, Descendant, and Midheaven or Nadir—even if they are on the cadent side of the angle. Traditionally, planets so placed are thought to manifest most potently in the circumstances indicated by the houses defined by those cusps. But judgment as to the relative potency of these positions is an individual call and varies from astrologer to astrologer.

Antiscions: A term usually applied to alternate signs such as Virgo and Scorpio which, on the rising of Libra, hold an equal distance from the horizon. Thus the 10th degree of Virgo will be 20 degrees from 0 Libra and will be the antiscion of the 20th degree of Scorpio. Similarly Gemini 9 is the antiscion of Leo 21; both are equidistant from 0 Cancer. (see Parallels)

Antivertex: The intersection of the Ecliptic with the three main mutually perpendicular local planes (that is, the Horizon, the Meridian, and the Prime Vertical) defines the Ascendant, Midheaven, and Vertex, respectively. The Vertex is the third angle and is found in the proximity of the Descendant. The Antivertex is opposite the Vertex and is found near the Ascendant. Some computerized astrological programs include the calculation of the Vertex and Antivertex. Studies have not found the Antivertex to be conspicuously significant, although some astrologers consider this point to be an auxiliary Ascendant and do use it.

APHELION: The point at which a planet or any other orbiting body is farthest from the Sun in its revolution.

APOGEE: This usually refers to that point in the orbit of the Moon, or any other planet, when it is at its greatest distance from Earth.

Application: The term used to describe the movement of one planet into exact aspect with another. There are three kinds:

1. Direct application; where two planets are moving forward but one is moving faster than the other overtaking it to form an aspect.

2. Retrograde application; where two planets are moving backward but one overtakes the other in a similar manner.

3. Mixed application; where one planet is moving direct

and the other is moving retrograde whereupon they mutually apply to each other. (see Separation)

AQUARIUS: Aquarius is the Fixed sign in the Air Triplicity. Fixed signs appear in the second month of each season and describe a general attitude type which is Introverted. Air signs project the function of thinking. Thus, more specifically, Aquarius describes the psychological function Introverted Thinking.

This is the second month of the winter season, usually the coldest time of the year. In earlier epochs this was the time of the year when one needed a friend and felt impelled to come to the aid of others in need. A desperate time of year. The question "what's it all about?" could certainly be stimulated by the harsh environment and limitations of this season conditioning humankind to introspection and search for meaning.

Thinking in Aquarius is not like the rather social chit-chatty sharing of information kind of thinking that Gemini does, nor is it like the linking-thinking, making connections, relating one thing with another, clarifying, explaining kind of thinking that goes on in Libra. Because it is introverted, Aquarian thinking seeks to understand outer circumstances by drawing upon inner images and subjective ideas. It has a greater capacity to deal with abstract ideas than do the other signs. It is a type of thinking which formulates questions, creates theories, and tends to be more geared to the future than to the present. Thus it frequently has a propensity to be progressive or avant-garde. Facts themselves are not of interest to the Aquarian as they are to the Libran. Facts may be collected as evidence or examples of a theory, but never for their own sake. It is the sort of thinking done by the scientist, the researcher, the theoretician, and often the ideologue.

A great American astrologer, Marc Edmund Jones, has said of Aquarius, "He is a seeker after guiding principles." And with regard to the idealism of Aquarius he also says, "The ideal shall never touch the real." The distant goal is always more appealing than the immediate situation.

This is one of the "sweet" signs, and those strongly identified with this sign are usually very casual and easy-going, not at all petty, and very likeable. They have a live and let live outlook and tend to accept people at face value. Unlike Leo, their opposite number, they are not egoistic, perhaps to a fault. They do not forget that their successes often depend on the people around them who may have participated in a successful project or effort. They give credit to the group or to others. Aquarians are often attracted to social causes, for they are lovers of humanity but they get very nervous if someone tries to get too close or makes special demands on them. Personal freedom is so very important. They are often accused of being detached and indifferent, and, in fact, they often are. And yet this is the sign of loyalty, for once they have formed a friendship or attachment with a person, a group, an idea, or a goal, they are reluctant to betray the ideal which will be found behind the attachment in the first place. Thus there is a persistent stubbornness in this sign; a resistance to change.

Aquarians love to tease and to play devil's advocate, often taking the opposing view in a discussion just for the sake of argument. They can be very perverse.

Arabian Parts (or Points): An Arabian system for assigning specialized significance to certain degrees of the Zodiac. This system of parts has fallen largely into disuse with the exception of one part, the Pars Fortuna or Part of Fortune, which is said to be a fortunate degree and the house it falls in a fortunate circumstance in the horoscope. This degree is found by adding to the Ascendant the position of the Moon and subtracting from that sum the position of the Sun (Ascendant + Moon−Sun). Any planet or point can be substituted for the Moon, or for both Moon and Sun, or for all three, producing hundreds of other parts. There is the Part of Marriage, the Part of Death, the Part of Pleasure, etc. This multiplicity reduces the whole exercise to absurdity.

ARIES: The meaning of the signs comes not from some distant constellation, but from what is happening in the Earth at the time the Sun is moving through that particular sign.

Because most of us live in steam-heated, air-conditioned houses or apartments, we have lost touch with the incredible jubilation that ancient humankind must have felt at the cessation of the long cold winter—that icy, dreary, depressing time when stores of food dwindled, the weak died off, and hunger enfeebled those who survived. Suddenly the first shoots of green would appear pushing through the snow that started to melt in the soft spring rains. The days began to last longer than the nights, and buoyant, balmy breezes began to blow. Spring! How exhilarating it must have been to those who had survived. How inspiring to their sense of adventure, and the courage to take a chance on climbing that distant mountain or crossing that river, pushing the known boundaries further and further in order to find a better life. This is the spirit of Aries; excitement, aspiration, enthusiasm, daring, joie de vivre.

No wonder it is at this time of year that we celebrate Easter, the Resurrection, the Easter egg, the bunny rabbit—all symbolic of rebirth and new life. It is at this time that Persephone returns from the underworld and brings verdant growth and flowering to the Earth once again.

Aries is the Cardinal sign of the fire Triplicity. It is the first sign of the Zodiac. It is initiated by the vernal equinox, that time of the year when the Sun is at the point on the ecliptic where the ecliptic and equator converge, and in its journey the Sun is heading north, above the equator toward the Tropic of Cancer. This is the first day of spring when the Earth once again experiences equal day and night, but now, the days will gradually get longer and longer until the summer solstice, the longest day. On this day, the day of the vernal equinox we say the Sun is in the zero degrees of Aries: the Zodiacal year has begun.

Because Aries occurs in the first month of spring it is a Cardinal sign, which means that the general attitude it projects is highly extroverted. It is also a Fire sign so the function it projects is feeling. Thus Aries is the sign of Extroverted Feeling. It looks outward with excitement and delight at the wonderful opportunities and adventure in the world. It is not introspective, it is not thoughtful. It wants action, it wants to do, to move. Aries is feeling, not as reaction, emotion, or response (which more appropriately belong with the Water signs), but as aspiration, enthusiasm, excitement, and exhilaration. It is the sign of the leader, the pioneer, the fool who goes where angels fear to tread, but whose courage and daring pave the way for more timid souls to follow.

Aries tends to be ego-driven and self-centered. But it is natural for this sign to operate strictly from self. It couldn't be the leader it is if it didn't. It is an "I" sign; "I AM." There is much courage in Aries—it is often combative, aggressive, fast, full of energy, impatient, impetuous, unthinking, and sometimes exceedingly naive.

ASCENDANT: The Ascendant is the degree of the Zodiac which is rising (coming up over the Horizon) at the time of birth. The Rising Sign and its degree are synonymous with the first house of the horoscope; that space more or less 30 degrees below the east Horizon.

Since a horoscope is a blending of many factors, no one point can be totally descriptive of an individual. But the Ascendant is one of the most important indicators not only of the physical appearance of the person but of her/his characteristics, traits, talents, and faults.

I believe the Ascendant describes the ego, which is defined by Jung as "the conscious standpoint," which sign in turn is the dominant function. In other words, the psychological function indicated by the Rising Sign sheds light on those gifts and talents most readily at hand, and also on the person's initial approach to things, on the perspective that person has on whatever may be happening in her/his life at any given moment. (see Houses)

ASPECTS: An aspect is a specific degree relationship between two bodies. The aspects between planets show how the principles identified by the planets merge, producing interesting results or effects. For instance, if we see Mercury as a princi-

18

ple of perception, the nature of that perception will be modified in the direction of a more sensitive, serious, perhaps more discriminating, practical, and realistic mode if Mercury is in aspect to Saturn. On the other hand perception will manifest in a more imaginative, fanciful, whimsical, or poetic direction if Mercury is in aspect to Neptune. Perception or thinking will be more analytical, probing, and obsessive with Mercury in aspect to Pluto, and more individualistic, unfettered, and perverse when in aspect to Uranus.

And so it is with all of the aspects between all of the planets; they modify each other.

When planets are 180 degrees apart, it's called an OPPOSITION. For instance: a planet in 5 degrees of Aries is exactly 180 away from a planet in 5 degrees of Libra. This is an exact opposition. However, we may still call this an opposition even if it is not exact. A certain "orb" of aspect is allowed, which varies with different astrologers. At the most, a 10 degree orb is acceptable to many astrologers. If one planet is in three degrees of Aries and the other Planet is in nine degrees of Libra, these two Planets are still within 10 degrees of the opposition aspect. Most astrologers would not consider a planet in five degrees of Aries to be in valid opposition to a planet in 18 degrees of Libra: the orb (18−5=13) is too wide.

Planets are said to be CONJUNCT (together) if within 0 to 10 degrees of each other (again the orb of allowance will vary).

The SQUARE is when planets are more or less 90 degrees apart.

The SEXTILE occurs when planets are more or less 60 degrees apart.

The TRINE has the planets 120 degrees apart, more or less.

The aspects described above are the five major aspects used by Ptolemy, an astronomer, astrologer, and mathematician from the second century AD. They are called the Ptolemaic Aspects. They are created by dividing the circle by one—close together within 10 degrees (conjunct), dividing the circle by two—180 degrees (opposition), by three—120 degrees (trine), by four—90 degrees (square), by six—60 degrees (sextile).

Nowadays most astrologers no longer think of the aspects between planets as being evil, malefic, or fortunate, benefic. They prefer to see certain aspects as difficult and others as easy.

The evaluation placed upon the most commonly used aspects, the Ptolemaic Aspects, is as follows:

CONJUNCTION: indicates activity.

OPPOSITION: indicates awareness and opportunity; sometimes conflict.

SQUARE: an aspect of construction and effort; difficult at times but in the end most rewarding.

These three aspects are often considered difficult or harsh, especially the square which generates much tension and stress. Handling difficulty forces us to develop resourcefulness and competence. As for the conjunction, the difficulty there depends much upon the planets involved, and the opposition can indicate wonderful opportunity, again depending on the planets involved and whatever supportive aspects there may be. Marc Jones has said these aspects are character building, strengthening.

TRINE: indicates momentum, unobstructed flow.

There may be ease, luck at times with this aspect

which is often pleasant but sometimes disastrous. The silver spoon may not be such a great boon as one might think.

SEXTILE: is an aspect of assistance, support, help. Very welcome at times but this too can encourage a tendency to drift.

The trine and sextile aspects may be supportive, helpful and often downright lucky, but they are conducive to coasting and may be character weakening.

Then there are many other aspects, minor aspects, less frequently used by astrologers. They are created by divisions of the above major aspects:

The Semi-sextile of 30 degrees separation—half a sextile.

The Quincunx or inconjunct of 150 degrees of separation—30 degrees short of an opposition.

These two aspects are said to signify growth or adjustment.

The Semi-square of 45 degrees separation—half a square.

The sesquare of 135 degrees separation—a square and a half.

These two aspects are thought by some astrologers to indicate stress or difficulty.

The wonderful astronomer-astrologer Kepler devised a quintile group of aspects which were multiples or divisions of a fifth of the circle—72 degrees.

The Quintile, 72 degrees.

This aspect is treated as an indication of talent.

THE FIVE MAJOR ASPECTS

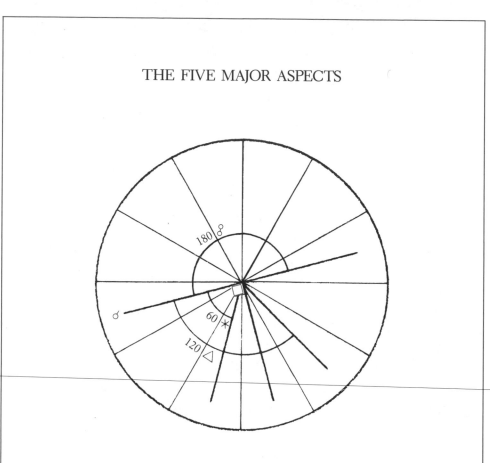

0° to 10° ☌ CONJUNCTION
180° ☍ OPPOSITION
60° ✶ SEXTILE
90° ☐ SQUARE
120° △ TRINE

The Bi-quintile—twice 72 degrees, or 144 degrees.

The Semi-quintile—half a quintile, or 36 degrees.

These two aspects may also have to do with talent for they are relatives of the quintile.

There is a division of the circle by seven called the Septile—51.42 degrees—which is sometimes used. It is called an aspect of fatality, and I am not certain why. It is an awkward number to use and difficult to pick out easily, so this aspect has been neglected by astrologers, including yours truly. But now computer programs can easily indicate when this aspect exists, so perhaps with more dedicated study its nature will be more adequately defined.

All aspects may be dexter or sinister. Dexter aspects are those made to preceding signs and sinister aspects are those made to succeeding signs. Thus the Sun in five degrees of Aries is in sinister sextile to a planet in five degrees of Gemini and in dexter sextile to a planet in five degrees of Aquarius. I do not believe there is a qualitative difference to be inferred based upon whether an aspect is dexter or sinister. It simply facilitates locating them.

ASTEROIDS: Small planets found in the solar system between the orbits of Mars and Jupiter, in the region now called the Asteroid Belt. There are at least 4,000 of these small bodies of varying shapes and sizes.

The first of these bodies was discovered by an Italian astronomer named Giuseppi Piazzi from the observatory at Palermo, Sicily, on January 1, 1801. Piazzi named this new planet after Ceres, the patron goddess of Sicily. Within the next six years three more asteroids were discovered. They were given the names Pallas, Juno, and Vesta by their astronomer discoverers. That is the custom: When a new planet, asteroid or comet is discovered it is named by its discoverer. These astronomers, to whom we are eternally grateful, have no idea that in naming a newly discovered body, they are identifying an archetype. Just as all of the other planets represent the same principles as the gods whose names they bear, so do the asteroids and the other most recently discovered planets.

Sometimes attempts are made to give a planet a name other than its appropriate one. It doesn't stick. Some celebrated astronomer wanted Ceres to be named Hera, the Greek name for Juno. That would not do at all, for Hera represents an entirely different principle. Eventually he gave up on his mission.

These four small planets are named for four great goddesses. That is to say they are facets of the feminine principle. It is an astonishing fact that of the ten bodies used in the horoscope, without the asteroids, only two are feminine: the Moon and Venus. All of the others are masculine. The asteroids represent aspects of the feminine principle that the Moon and Venus do not, cannot convey. Briefly put, the feminine as defined by the Moon and Venus is seen as an emotional weathervane, completely dominated by her menstrual cycle (Moon) or object of gratification and pleasure (Venus). Come on now. We women just aren't accepting that limited definition of our being any longer. The feminine is much more than that, and at long last, the asteroids are here to identify and to demonstrate the remarkable facets of the feminine, many of which in large part have been usurped by the masculine.

Ceres, Pallas, and Vesta are the largest asteroids in the

CERES

♀

MOTHER

SYMBOLS

poppy
plough & sickle
crane

seed
torch
cornucopia

FUNDAMENTAL HUMAN NEED
Food

MANIFESTATION IN PERSONALITY TRAITS

hard worker
caring
nurturing
productive

helpful
sharing
serving
natural

PLACES OF MANIFESTATION

rural life
farms
kitchens, pantries
restaurants

nurseries
communes
gardens

MANIFESTATION IN OCCUPATION

farmer, laborer
producer
waiter
nurse, doctor
service occupations
social worker
union leader

herbalist, botanist
chef, cook, baker
nutritionist
veterinarian
helping professions
witch, healer

*MANIFESTATIONS IN THINGS, ACTIONS,
AND ABSTRACT CONCEPTS*

all foods
cultivation
grief at human suffering
bountiful earth
civil disobedience
GNP

life-promoting
concern, care, healing
labor, as in birth
labor, as in to produce
peaceful protest

NEGATIVE MANIFESTATION

workaholic
inadequate care, concern
strike, malcontent
food poisoning
unemployment

drought, famine
malnutrition
diminished productivity
stunted growth
diminished GNP

THE ASTEROIDS—AREAS OF MANIFESTATION
All four are generally symbolized by mystery and the serpent
All four represent fundamental human needs

JUNO

♀

WIFE

SYMBOLS

pomegranate

peacock & cuckoo

the winds

veil

flowers

scepter

FUNDAMENTAL HUMAN NEED
Clothing

MANIFESTATION IN PERSONALITY TRAITS

charming

disarming

hospitable

gracious

stylish

diplomatic

seductive

cooperative

PLACES OF MANIFESTATION

social life

fashion shows

hotels, hostels

weddings

hosting, partying

diplomatic circles

cultural events

MANIFESTATION IN OCCUPATION

meteorologist

fashion designer

diplomat

mediator

stylist

secretary, office wife

maitre d'

environmentalist

decorator

hostess, host

mannequin, model

wife, helpmate, aide

receptionist

MANIFESTATION IN THINGS, ACTIONS,
AND ABSTRACT CONCEPTS

civility

enhancement of life

disarmament, cooperation

refinement, delicacy

make-up, toilette

marriage, childbirth

lifestyle

gracious living

chivalry, courtship

smallness, fragility

atmosphere

NEGATIVE MANIFESTATION

violation of the powerless

rape, incest, pornography

torrential rainstorms

outrage at powerlessness

juvenile delinquency

child abuse, wife beating

environmental pollution

hurricanes and tornadoes

terrorist acts

vandalism

VESTA

$\maltese$

SISTER

SYMBOLS

flame	altar
globe	donkey
vestibule	hearth

FUNDAMENTAL HUMAN NEED
Shelter

MANIFESTATION IN PERSONALITY TRAITS

conservative	conventional
traditional	trustworthy
patriotic	security-conscious
safety-conscious	purist

PLACES OF MANIFESTATION

home, family life	historical foundations
sanctuaries, embassies	insurance firms
investment firms	investigative agencies
ethnic organizations	

MANIFESTATION IN OCCUPATION

stockbroker	security guard
insurance salesperson	mapmaker
locksmith	investigator
nun, priest, rabbi, etc.	licensing, real estate
police, armed services	lobbyist
archivist	custodian, trustee
genealogist	

MANIFESTATION IN THINGS, ACTIONS, AND ABSTRACT CONCEPTS

security, safety, protection	insurance, pension
contracts, treaties	licensing, accreditation
locks, keys, walls, fences	turf, boundaries, borders
ethnicity, heritage	vested interests
family, belonging, clan, group	clandestine operations, spying
CIA, FBI, investigators	

NEGATIVE MANIFESTATION

vigilantism	Mafia (The Family)
fear of change	KKK, Nazism
zealot, fanatic	selfish vested interests
hostility to strangers	ethnic and racial purity
questionable credibility	restrictive fundamentalism

27

PALLAS

☿

DAUGHTER

SYMBOLS

olive

owl

spider

shield & spear

horse

distaff & flute

FUNDAMENTAL HUMAN NEED
Industry

MANIFESTATION IN PERSONALITY TRAITS

autonomous

resourceful

inventive

self-sufficient

efficient

ingenious

self-determined

self-controlled

PLACES OF MANIFESTATION

urban life

think-tanks

design studios

industrial centers

laboratories

research centers

court houses

MANIFESTATION IN OCCUPATION

economist

engineer

designer, technician, tool maker

inventor

computer programmer

efficiency expert

artists & craftspeople

lawyer, judge

composer, choreographer

strategist

city planner

MANIFESTATION IN THINGS, ACTIONS, AND ABSTRACT CONCEPTS

economics

coordination

energy saving devices

pattern perception

immune system

cottage industry

excellence

labor saving devices

gestalt perception

DNA genetic code

birth control

NEGATIVE MANIFESTATION

autism

perceptive distortions

miscarriage of justice

breakdown of immune system

wasted materials & energy

dyslexia

inefficiency

lack of autonomy

severe austerity

difficulty solving problems

Asteroid Belt, but there are several asteroids that are larger than Juno, though they were discovered more than forty years later than she was. At any rate, these first four asteroids stood alone as new and accepted members of the family of planets in the solar system for forty years, until in 1845, along with the discovery of Neptune, asteroid discovery resumed with gusto.

Little attention was paid them by astrologers for the simple reason that ephemerides, or tables of their daily positions in the zodiac, were not available. Calculation of their orbits for astrologers' use was a Herculean task and was not attempted until 1972 when, because of the development of the computer, that task was no longer so formidable and I commissioned astronomer George Climlas to create ephemerides for these bodies. *The First Ephemerides of the Asteroids* was published in January 1973; thus, at long last, astrologers were able to study these small bodies in order to determine their significance. They have added a fascinating new dimension to the art of astrology.

Ephemerides are now available for any asteroid one wants to study. But the only really thoroughly researched asteroids are the first four: Ceres, Pallas, Juno, and Vesta, and they will be described individually in their appropriate places in this dictionary.

ASTRONOMICAL UNIT: One Astronomical Unit (AU) is the distance from Sun to Earth. The distances of all planets from the Sun are measured in Astronomical Units, or parts of Astronomical Units. (see Bode's Law)

Barren Signs: Those signs that are said to deny the capacity to conceive in a woman or which indicate sterility in a man when placed upon the cusp of the fifth House. They are Aries, Gemini, Leo, and Virgo. This is a medieval concept and its validity has not been statistically corroborated in our time.

Bestial Signs: Aries—the Ram; Taurus—the Bull; Leo—the Lion; Sagittarius—the Centaur; and Capricorn—the goat. No, they are not beastly characteristics that these signs describe; the term simply refers to the animals for which they are named. They are totem animals in a sense, and those born with one or another of these signs prominent seem to have a special fondness for their totem animal.

Besieged: Another medieval term used to describe the placement of a planet between two benefics or two malefics. If the planet was besieged by two so-called benefic planets that was thought to be good, and when it was besieged by two so-called malefic planets, that was thought to be bad, or as they used to love to say, evil. Nowadays we do not place a positive or negative value on such a configuration, but we try to understand what it requires.

Birth: Astrologers differ on the definition of the moment of birth. Some think it is the moment of the cutting of the cord, others claim it is the first cry. It is whatever is considered to be that moment when the baby is a separate entity, no longer using the support system provided by the mother's placenta and womb; when it is breathing on its own. Whatever the case may be, let's not worry about it, for it is seldom that a birth is recorded at the exact moment of the first cry or the scissors' snip. Most astrologers are glad if they get a birthtime that is correct within ten minutes.

Bitter Signs: Aries, Leo, and Sagittarius, because they are said to be hot and fiery. There is a self-centered aspect to these fire signs, and if natives of these signs perceive themselves to be neglected or ignored, they may indeed feel a little "bitter."

BODE'S LAW: An observation first made by Titius in 1751, but given prominence by Bode in 1776. Titius noted that there is a peculiar and regular proportion in the separation of the planets from each other; the distance from Mercury to Venus, Venus to Earth, Earth to Mars — and he remarked upon the significant and unexpectedly wide gap between Mars and Jupiter. He surmised that that space was occupied by hitherto undiscovered moons of Mars and, perhaps, Jupiter. Bode, a contemporary of Titius, was also concerned about the spacing of the planets. He seized upon the numerical relationship which Titius discovered and really promoted it. He did not doubt that undiscovered planets existed between Mars and Jupiter as well as beyond Saturn. Titius' progression came to be known as

Bode's law. It worked as follows: Start with the numbers zero, three, and six, doubling each succeeding number (i.e. 6, 12, etc.). If four is added to each number and it is then divided by 10, the figure thus obtained gives the approximate distance from the Sun in Astronomical Units of the then known planets. (see Astronomical Unit)

PLANET	TITIUS' PROGRESSION	ACTUAL DISTANCE (AU)
Mercury	$(0+4)/10 = 0.4$	0.387
Venus	$(3+4)/10 = 0.7$	0.723
Earth	$(6+4)/10 = 1.0$	1.00
Mars	$(12+4)/10 = 1.6$	1.524
Ceres	$(24+4)/10 = 2.8$	2.767
Jupiter	$(48+4)/10 = 5.2$	5.203
Saturn	$(96+4)/10 = 10.0$	9.539
Uranus	$(192+4)/10 = 19.6$	19.8
Neptune	$(384+4)/10 = 38.8$	30.6
Pluto	$(768+4)/10 = 77.2$	39.4

This law stimulated a renewed zest in planetary observation and the search for new planets. The first to be discovered was Uranus in 1781, almost exactly where it was expected to be. Then, in 1801, the first asteroid, Ceres, was discovered at precisely the point where a missing planet was supposed to be, 2.8 AU. As you can see, the system fails to work in the case of Neptune and Pluto, but some astronomers believe that Bode's law or a similar system will work if certain masses and distances are taken into account.

Brahe, Tycho: Astronomer, 1546–1601. Famous for his accurate observations of the positions of the stars and planets.

CANCER: Cancer is the fourth sign of the Zodiac. It is the Cardinal Water sign. This sign is initiated by the summer solstice. It begins in the first month of the summer season. It is the time of the longest day and the shortest night.

Since Cardinal signs manifest in a general attitude that is extroverted, and Water signs express the function intuition, Cancer identifies Extroverted Intuition. That is not to say that this sign is noisy, intrusive, or always calling attention to itself. Cancer is often very shy, sensitive, and self-protective, but the intuitions it expresses are stimulated by *external* events or objects. A black cat crossing one's path; being reminded of a long-lost friend by a billboard poster and, upon calling that friend finding that that s/he has been looking for *you*; going down one street instead of another on impulse and running into someone one wanted to know or meet; and even at times quite dramatic experiences such as canceling an airplane reservation for no apparent reason only to find out later that the plane has crashed, all represent the nature of Cancer's intuition. Individuals with a strong emphasis of the sign Cancer in their charts will be highly intuitive—perhaps even psychic.

The great American astrologer Marc Edmund Jones calls the sign Cancer the sign of the prophet. There is a talent in this sign for seeing or sensing the potentials or possibilities in an object, a person, or a situation. Individuals in business with a strong emphasis in this sign are way ahead of their colleagues in perceiving the trends or direction of public interest, and in tuning in to that which the public will respond—in fashion, politics, fads, interest, entertainment, and concerns.

Since Cancer is ruled by the Moon, it is perhaps the most emotionally responsive of the signs. Emotions often accompany intense flashes of intuitive perception (ESP). And, like emotions, intuitions are inadvertent, or not subject to control. They are reactive responses. They require no judgment and no evaluation; they simply present themselves. One simply 'knows' without knowing how one knows.

There is a mothering tendency in this sign, most obviously expressed in the literal feeding and accompanying emotional nurturance a mother gives the helpless infant—liquid nourishment. After all, this sign rules the breasts and other containers; jugs, bottles, gourds, and the various liquids that fill them.

Cancer people make marvelous teachers. This is because of their nurturing manner and their gift of perception of potential. On the other hand, if the perception of potential flags, that very nurturing individual may drop a person or an interest like a hot potato. For all its mothering, the sign Cancer can be very ruthless.

Aside from emotion and intuition, the sign Cancer is notable for a tendency to collect things, often containers (a man I met with a number of planets in Cancer, had a room full of lighted bookshelves filled with Venetian glassware—containers of course) or other collectibles tinged with sentimental value, such as baseball cards, comic books, antique cars, or whatever. This must have something to do with the sentimental attachment to things of the past and the emotions connected with childhood memories.

Cancer individuals are said to be homebodies but that is not necessarily so: They do have a tendency to make a home of wherever they may be, perhaps to create a more "homey" atmosphere of the sterile hotel or motel room they occupy in some distant part of the world. (Like their animal symbol, the crab, they carry their home with them.) And they are often very self-protective (feeling vulnerable like the crab when it loses its shell), and protective of others with whom they feel kinship.

Of course the Moon rules this sign, for rhythmical tides of the oceans are controlled by the Moon's cycle, as is the female menstrual cycle.

CAPRICORN: Capricorn is the tenth sign of the Zodiac. It is Cardinal Winter sign and the element it expresses is Earth, Cardinal Earth, which, after our system, identifies the psychological function Extroverted Sensation.

The Sun enters the sign Capricorn at the winter solstice, December 21st. After the autumnal equinox in September, sunrises occur later and sunsets earlier on each succeeding day until the winter solstice, the day of the longest night. In a sense this long night symbolizes a time of the greatest darkness and despair and yet it is also the time of the renewal of hope, for the winter solstice is the turning point of the Sun. It will now begin to climb higher and higher in the sky and each succeeding sunrise will be earlier and each sunset later, until finally it is spring once again. So in this very dark time, there is cause for celebration, for jubilation. This is the time of the many festivals of lights, celebrated since ancient times by giant bonfires, the Yule Log, Chanukah candles, and Christmas trees lit with candles or colored lights and decorated with mistletoe. All these are examples of sympathetic magic, encouraging the weakened Sun to be reborn, and expressing the hope of survival after the dark night. Here, at the darkest time, things have reached their low point and can only get better. That is what we celebrate at this time of the year.

The characteristics associated with this sign are the following: experience through the senses—keen awareness of physical surroundings, responsiveness to the atmosphere and environment, discrimination, critical observation, and reality perception. This is a no-nonsense kind of sign, earthy, practical, sensible, materialistic, and often ambitious. Capricorn people are good trouble-shooters and crisis handlers, inclined to find solutions to problems rather than than to cry over spilled milk. They know that it takes practice and experience to develop skill and so Capricorn natives accept the proposition that if you are going to do something, do it right or do it over again till you get it right.

Whereas its opposite number, Cancer, tends to be exceedingly emotional (flowing water), Capricorn inclines to control emotions (frozen water). It is more prosaic, pragmatic, stoic, and looks for practical solutions to problems. Whereas Cancer is tuned in to the invisible, the intangible, to the possibilities, Capricorn is aware of realities, of limitations, and of structure and form.

Because of having to deal with reality, Capricorn has the capacity to develop great skill; skill in using the body, as in dance and athletics; or skill in mechanics; skill in handling materials, tools, and instruments. Because of their ability to discriminate Capricorn natives tend to be perfectionists; they are their own worst critics.

The lusty and agile mountain goat is the animal symbol for Capricorn. Like the goat Capricorn is a climber, often literally (rock or mountain climbing) and frequently symbolically—ambitious for achievement—climbing the social or professional ladder. But failure in the attainment of their goals often means being subject to severe depression.

This sign is ruled by Saturn and because Saturn is Cronus, or time, timing is very important for Capricorn. There is also an appreciation of things which have stood the test of time, of old things, antiques. And for all its seriousness and sensitivity, some of the most successful comedians and clowns, for whom a sense of timing is very important, have a large dose of Capricorn in their make-up. This is an old-young, young-old sign, in which people often look younger as they get older and develop a merrier or lighter outlook on life with the passage of time.

Caput Draconis: The Dragon's Head or the Moon's ascending node; the point in the Zodiac where the Moon's orbit crosses the Ecliptic heading northward. The opposite point is the

Cauda Draconis or the Dragon's Tail or the Moon's descending node, where she is heading southward. These are more commonly called the North Node and the South Node.

Cardinal Cross: (see Angles)

CARDINAL SIGNS: These are Aries, Cancer, Libra, and Capricorn. Cardinal means fundamental. Each of these signs is of a different element: Fire, Water, Air, and Earth. But what they do have in common is the fact that they are the signs that initiate each season. The first month of spring, summer, fall and winter.

With the onset of each season, attention is directed outward, captivated by the changes the new season brings. The Cardinal signs all project an air of excitement at newness, at change. Recall your own weariness of winter and longing for spring, the heady feeling you experience as the chilly winds of winter become the silky, satiny breezes of spring, and you notice the hardy little buds of green pushing their heads through the snow on the ground and swelling the branches on the trees. And recall when the Earth shifts into its summer mode; that, too, is exciting, generating thoughts of vacation time, going to the beach, basking in the Sun, and perhaps trying to get a tan. But then we weary of summer and begin to long for the stimulation of fall, its chill crispness, its clarity, and the riotous color changes in the foliage. And as fall becomes too damp and dreary and the trees become barren skeletons, we even welcome the snows of winter once again; the Earth in her winter wonderland garb, the coming of the holidays.

The excitement of these Earth changes has a parallel in

the psyche of humankind. These signs indicate a general attitude that is extroverted, in the sense that attention is captivated by current crises, objective matters and facts, by the immediate situation in which one finds oneself. The matters that these signs are involved with are fast-moving, current, and need to be attended to at once, if not yesterday.

Since the four elements represent the four psychological functions, we may then designate Aries as representing Extroverted Feeling; Cancer as representing Extroverted Intuition; Libra as representing Extroverted Thinking; and Capricorn as representing Extroverted Sensation.

Cazimi: This is when a planet is within 17 minutes of the Sun. It is a conjunction of course, but a very close one. Supposedly this condition indicates unusual brilliance with regard to the matters that the planet comprises. Another fabulous claim. (see Combust)

CERES: Ceres was discovered on January 1st, 1801, by the astronomer Guiseppe Piazzi from the observatory at Palermo, Sicily. He thought he had discovered THE missing body that was believed to be located at the 2.8 AU distance from the Sun, between the orbits of Mars and Jupiter. But it was instead the first and largest of the first four asteroids which were discovered in a six year period from 1801 to 1807.

Since a planet is the same archetype as the god or goddess whose name it bears, there was nothing for it but that this body should be named Ceres, after the goddess of the grain and harvest, the patron goddess of Sicily, as it happened. Piazzi gave her that name, coincidentally identifying an astrological archetype.

Astronomically, Ceres is the largest of the asteroids, about 480 miles in diameter. Of the four asteroids, she has the least eccentric orbit, the slowest rotation period—about nine hours—completes her orbit in about four and one half years, and is inclined to the ecliptic 10 and one half degrees.

Mythologically, Ceres is the goddess of the grain and the harvest, mother of Persephone, the beautiful maiden who was carried off to the underworld by Pluto. Grief-stricken at her loss, Ceres refused to permit even one stalk of grain to grow. She went on strike, so to speak, and demanded that her child be returned to her. A deal was finally struck (a little collective bargaining?), and Persephone was at last permitted to spend the better portion of the year above ground with her mother and the remainder of the year in the underworld with Pluto. This story symbolizes the natural cycle of birth, flowering, harvest, and death followed by rebirth which is metaphorically analogous to the experience of all living things.

Ceres is the principle of productivity. She is Mother Earth (Not to be confused with the Moon whom we might call Mother Water). Ceres gives solid form to things she produces. She is labor, work, productivity, and the caring that goes into the effort to make things grow. Unlike the Moon, an emotional, responsive and reactive principle, Ceres is an earthy, practical, reality principle. There is a cooperative connection between these two, the Moon and Ceres, for without water things will not grow, but without solid matter, without earth, things cannot be given form.

She has to do with literally all aspects of food: farming, cooking, serving, storing, selling, marketing, its nutritional aspect, and its absence—hunger and famine.

Because she is a productive principle, Ceres is also involved with labor, plentiful work and productivity, or its absence, unemployment. She has to do with labor unions and with labor-management relationships. She has to do with the weapon of labor—strike. Her myth actually tells us this: Ceres went on strike and refused to produce when Persephone was abducted.

Giving birth is called labor. That which we labor to produce we care about, and so Ceres is a nurturing, caring principle. Ceres aspects often involve grief at human suffering as Ceres suffered and grieved when her beloved daughter was taken from her. In this guise, Ceres is the nurse, and one often finds that she is prominent in the charts of nurses and doctors, and deeply involved with health and hospital services—the caring professions and services.

She does serve, and is often the indicator of service occupations, such as a waitress, an answering service worker, a shopping service, or a floor-sanding service, an executive at a banking service, a stockbroker who services your portfolio, etc.

The nature of her caring, productivity, and service is conditioned by the sign she happens to be found in at birth. In Leo, she could indicate a theatrical producer or production, dramatizing food (preparing it for the photographer) as I have found; in Gemini she could indicate book production, a telephone answering service, or writing cookbooks; in Pisces there may be a development with fish farming or piscatorial cuisine; in Aries she could deal with the production of military weapons or the logistical problems of feeding an army; in Taurus, the Venus-ruled sign (Venus is sugar), I know of several cases where the person is a pastry or confectionery chef. And so on. The sign determines the mode of expression of the planet. Please note how different these Ceres matters are from those that concern the Moon and Venus.

With Vesta, Ceres shares the rulership of the sign Virgo.

Chart Comparison: This is a system of synastry in which the planets and key points in one person's chart are compared with those of another person. The interplay between the planets of each person's chart can reveal much about the harmonies and stresses between two people.

Chronocrator: The planet that is said to rule a certain period of time in a person's life. There are several systems for determining this. The best known is the following: that which allots the first seven years to the Moon, the next eight years to Mercury, the next nine to Venus, add 10 for the Sun, 11 more for Mars, 12 to Jupiter and the last 13 to Saturn. The sum of these is 70. Should the life exceed these limits Uranus takes the next 14 years, Neptune the following 15 years, and Pluto the next 16 years. You can end up with 105, if you are lucky.

The first seven of these correspond with the "Seven Ages of Man" described in Shakespeare's play *As You Like It.* Significant? I don't know. It's fun.

Circle, in astronomy and astrology: Any circle, the plane (or level) of which passes through the center of the Earth, thereby dividing it in half, is a *great* circle.

A *small* circle is any circle the plane of which does *not* pass through the center of the earth.

The three great circles of horizon, equator, and ecliptic are the main circles of reference for locating a planet's position relative to any place on Earth. The ecliptic is the great circle that is the earth's path around the sun. This is the circle in the vicinity of which we find the constellations of the zodiac.

Climacteral Periods: Every seventh and ninth year from birth. These are based on the motions of the Moon which repeats its squares and trines every seventh and ninth year, respectively. Astrologers rarely pay any attention to this in our time.

Collection of Light: This is when a third planet is in aspect to two other planets which are inconjunct (150 degrees apart) or not in major aspect to each other. Nevertheless, the planet which is in aspect to both, "collects their light," and links them.

Colors and Patterns associated with the Signs:

Aries: red
Taurus: pink and citron
Gemini: multi-colors
Cancer: green and silver
Leo: orange and gold
Virgo: black or dark blue with spots
tiny, delicate pattern
Libra: pastel colors
Scorpio: deep red, dark brown
Sagittarius: purple, stripes, and spots
Capricorn: earth tones, florals, black
Aquarius: white, aquamarine
Pisces: lavender, lilac

Combust: A planet is combust when it is within eight degrees 30 minutes of the body of the Sun. A very close conjunction. Since the Sun's orb extends 17 degrees, all planets within that distance are said to be conjunct the Sun. There are various medieval opinions about this condition. Some say it points to an exceptional brilliance and others that it has a withering effect on perception. I think it merely indicates an intensified self-centeredness.

COMETS: Comets are bodies orbiting the Sun, most of which develop extended luminous tails as they near the Sun. They are described nowadays as "dirty snowballs." Long thought to be portents of evil affecting great changes in the Earth, the atmosphere, and the affairs of men. This is another medieval view. I know of no study that validates this claim; until the past few years we have had no ephemerides of comets' orbits and have not been able to pay the close attention that is required to identify the activity of an object. This is a research that should be and will be done.

Common Signs: (see Mutable Signs)

Composite Charts: An attempt at synastry. In the opinion of this astrologer, a very weird and improbable concept. It is a kind of relationship chart in which the midpoint is taken between the two Suns, the two Moons, the two Mercurys, the two Venuses, etc. and a chart is constructed using the midpoint between the two Midheavens, taken for selected latitude. It is a chart that never happened and therefore has no basis in reality or time. It destroys the integrity and separate identity of both individuals and it endows this third entity, this composite chart, with gifts that neither party possesses by putting planets into signs that often do not appear in either of the two birth charts involved. This is an impossibility for we cannot use what we do not have. I much prefer chart comparison as a more valid approach to relationship or synastry. (see Chart Comparison)

Computers: Recent high-tech developments that have produced inexpensive personal computers have put the practice of astrology within reach of anybody with enough money to buy one. Programs have been written which perform with speed, ease, and accuracy all of the labors of the professional astrologers of the past. It is true that because of the computer, the mathematical and technical aspects of chart calculation and construction are no longer a barrier to those who may feel inept in these areas. The real skill of the astrologer, however, lies in the depth of understanding of the elements of chart interpretation. It is doubtful that a computer program of chart interpretation can ever replace the experienced astrologer.

It is to be hoped that computer programs will facilitate research and may one day help to establish the validity of astrology.

Conception: It may be significant, but who knows the exact moment of conception? Ptolemy proposed a formula for determining the moment of conception, but if it really worked or was really relevant, we would all be using it, wouldn't we? We don't.

Configuration: This may be a single aspect or it may refer to a specific combination of aspects involving two or more planets. A configuration called a Grand Cross occurs when two planets oppose each other and then, at approximately 90 degrees from one of these bodies, another opposing pair of planets forms a cross with the first pair. A configuration in which two or more planets oppose each other and one or more

45

CONFIGURATIONS

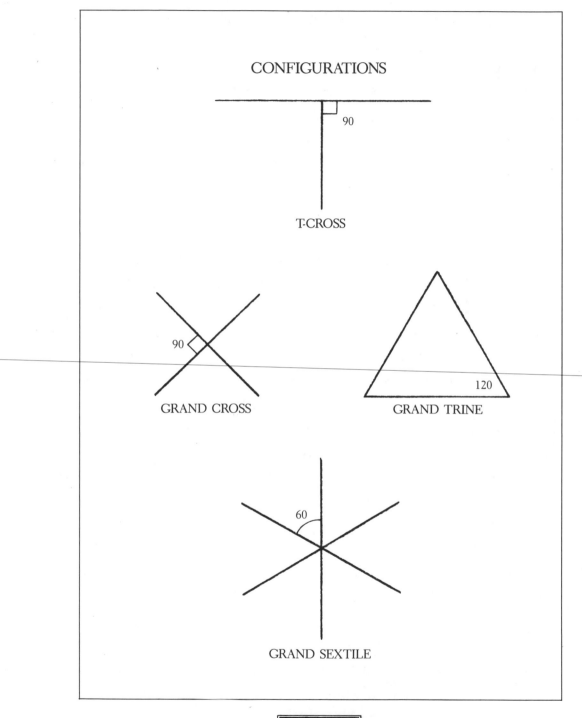

T-CROSS

GRAND CROSS

GRAND TRINE

GRAND SEXTILE

other planets are at right angles to the opposition is called a T-Cross. Three or more planets separated from each other by 120 degrees at three points in the heavens form a configuration called a Grand Trine, and when there are three oppositions separated by more or less 60 degrees, this creates a configuration called a Grand Sextile. (see Aspects)

Conjunction: One of the major aspects. (see Aspects)

Constellations: Constellations are star groups. Ancient astronomers perceived patterns in clusters of stars and gave them names. Those constellations of interest to astrologers are the ones found on the ecliptic, the path of the earth orbit around the Sun—the constellations of the Zodiac.

Copernicus, Nicholas: (1473 – 1543) A Polish monk who proposed a heliocentric model of the universe. Concerning his view of the cosmos he wrote: "In the middle of all sits the sun enthroned . . . He is rightly called the Lamp, the Mind, the Ruler of the universe . . . the sun sits upon a royal throne ruling his children the planets which circle round him."

Around 1529 he wrote a general description of his heliocentric cosmology. In his new model the earth not only revolved around the sun but also rotated daily on its axis. These ideas were new to his contemporaries but not to history. An earlier astronomer Aristarchus of Samos, first outlined them in the third century BC, but his work was lost.

Cosmobiology: A technique of astrological analysis devised by Reinhold Ebertin and based on the work of a German ballistics officer named Alfred Witte, who made considerable use of midpoints and introduced a number of "hypothetical planets," whatever they are. Witte gave these "planets" names and supposedly they have orbits too, but they cannot be seen. Ebertin adopted most of Witte's system, but used neither his invisible planets nor his house system. Ebertin called his system of interpretation through the use of midpoints "cosmobiology." Many astrologers are extremely dedicated to the system. I have not found that it contributes any information that cannot be obtained with the more traditional methods.

CUCKOO BIRD Since somewhere in this book we speak of the eagle as Jupiter's bird, I think it is only fair to have a look at the cuckoo which is Juno's bird. Besides, it's interesting.

The mother cuckoo lays her eggs in the nests of often much smaller birds, one in each nest. The stepmother bird hatches the orphan and the little cuckoo proceeds to roll the other eggs out of the nest, thereby becoming the only chick to be fed by the foster parents. These young cuckoos have such compelling cries that the foster parent birds work their wings to the bone trying to feed the young impostors. The cuckoo is rather a large bird and can in short order become even larger than the hard working little bird who thinks it is its mother.

The cuckoo is Juno's bird, one of her mythological emblems. The story of her marriage, as Robert Graves tells it, is that Jupiter, wishing to seduce Juno, disguised himself as a piteous cuckoo. She took the poor creature to her breast to comfort and warm, at which point Jupiter became himself and ravished her. She was thus shamed into marrying him. This marriage that began with Jupiter's trickery and his conquest of Juno surely represents the usurpation of feminine power in the beginning of the Aries Age. Graves says Jupiter could be correctly caricatured as the cuckoo, for he threw all of the other deities out of the nest! Graves also compared Jupiter in his cuckoo disguise to the mainland Greeks who came to the island of Crete as fugitives and found refuge and employment in the royal guard of this stronghold of the Great Goddess. These "cuckoo chicks" proceeded to create a conspiracy and seize the kingdom.

Culmination: When a planet arrives at the cusp of the Midheaven, the highest point in the chart. When natal planets by progression reach the Midheaven, the qualities that they signify will begin to manifest more directly in one's profession or career, will have greater impact on one's public image. When a transiting planet culminates, it, too, will for a time be a factor in the person's professional life.

Culmination is a term which is also used to indicate when any aspect between two planets becomes exact. This is when the activity indicated by the aspect is at its maximum.

CUSP: The beginning or edge of a house or a sign. The beginning of a sign is always zero degrees of that sign; the beginning of a house is more explicitly determined by birth time and by the house system the astrologer is using. Contingent on birth time and house system, the house cusps may be any degree from zero to 30 of any sign of the Zodiac.

Cycle: This usually refers to cycles of planetary conjunctions. But there are interesting cycles of planetary stations in the various signs which present some fascinating rhythms. There are cycles of Sun spots, cycles of eclipses. There are all kinds of terrestrial cycles for which adequate research may eventually establish an astrological connection.

Decant or Decanate: There are 30 degrees in every sign. A decanate is 10 degrees or one third of 30. Every sign has three decanates. Medieval astrologers assigned a slightly different mode of manifestation of the sign in each of the decanates. Most modern astrologers do not bother with using the decanates in their analysis.

Declination: The distance of any planet or place from the Celestial Equator, whether north or south, measured in degrees, minutes, and seconds. The plane of the Ecliptic (along which the Sun and planets travel) is not parallel with that of the equator, thus every part of the ecliptic has declination except the beginning of Aries or Libra because at 0 Aries and 0 Libra, Ecliptic and Equator meet.

Decreasing in Light: All planets decrease in light when they approach the Sun after having passed their point of opposition to it. Venus and Mercury decrease in light as they go nearer to the Sun after having reached their greatest elongation. The Moon decreases from full to new. To decrease in light means that whatever was accumulated during the time of increase in light must now be dispersed, spread about, made use of, applied. It is like knowledge accumulated over time that may now be made use of in life. Increase is like approaching flowering; decrease is like a time of seeding and dispersal. One state is not better than the other, it is merely different.

Degree: The 30th part of a sign or the 360th part of a circle. Every degree is divided into 60 minutes.

Delineation: A term used to indicate the analysis of a horoscope.

Denderah Zodiac: A representation of the Zodiac found in the temple at Denderah, Egypt, reputedly dating from the fourth millennium BC.

Descendant: The west angle or the cusp of the seventh house. (see Houses)

Detriment: A planet is in its detriment when it is found in the sign opposite the one it rules, such as:

Planet	Rules	Detriment
Sun	Leo	Aquarius
Moon	Cancer	Capricorn
Mercury	Gemini	Sagittarius
Venus	Taurus	Scorpio
Mars	Aries	Libra
(Ceres & Vesta	Virgo	Pisces)
(Pallas & Juno	Libra	Aries)
Jupiter	Sagittarius	Gemini
Saturn	Capricorn	Cancer
Uranus	Aquarius	Leo
Neptune	Pisces	Virgo
Pluto	Scorpio	Taurus

For balance we have included the asteroids as rulers of Virgo and Libra. However, to call these sign positions of planets their "detriment" should be looked upon as another nonsensical medieval designation. For think how useful a lawyer might find his Mars in Libra (fighting for justice), or how intensely creativity is enhanced for the artist with Venus in Scorpio? And think of the unusual number of notable scientists, theoreticians, and writers who were born with the Sun in Aquarius.

Dexter/Sinister: (see Aspects)

Dichotomy: Cut in half. A term applied to the Moon when in the first and third quarters, whereupon her disc appears to be only half luminous.

Dignities and Debilities—of Planets: This is an archaic technique to assign positive or negative significance to the planets in accordance with the sign they happen to be in at birth or are transiting in the heavens. It is of dubious value and or validity. And since new planets (and asteroids) have been discovered since the system was assigned, that system has been thrown off balance and has lost whatever meaning it was thought to have had.

But for the sake of history, the following is a list of the so-called dignities and debilities of the planets.

ESSENTIAL DIGNITIES

Determined by sign and by exaltation. When a planet is in the sign opposite that of its exaltation, it is said to be in its fall.

Planet	Rules	Exalted in	Falls in
Sun	Leo	Aries	Libra
Moon	Cancer	Taurus	Scorpio

52

Mercury	Gemini	Aquarius	Leo
Venus	Taurus	Pisces	Virgo
Mars	Aries	Capricorn	Cancer
Jupiter	Sagittarius	Cancer	Capricorn
Saturn	Capricorn	Libra	Aries

Uranus rules Aquarius—exaltation and fall unknown

Neptune Rules Pisces—exaltation and fall unknown

Ceres and Vesta rule Virgo—exaltation and fall unknown

Juno and Pallas rule Libra—exaltation and fall unknown

Pluto rules Scorpio—exaltation and fall unknown

ACCIDENTAL DIGNITIES

Determined by birth time. A planet is dignified if it is in an angle at birth, that is, in the first, fourth, seventh, or tenth houses. But it is said to be falling when it is in the third, sixth, ninth, or twelfth houses.

A planet elevated above all the others (highest in the chart) is said to be dignified.

Directions: A technique for moving the planets after the birth which permits the identification of times of major changes or new developments in a person's life. The contemporary term used for this action is "progressing the chart." (see Progressions)

Dispositor: In a horoscope, the planet which rules a given sign is known as the dispositor of all the other planets found in that sign at birth. Mars, as ruler of Aries, is the dispositor of any planets located in Aries. Venus, which rules Taurus, is the dispositor of the planets found in Taurus, and so on. This is a way of determining one or two of the most significant principles in one's life. For instance, let's say the following is a list of planets in a horoscope and the signs in which they are found:

Sun, Mercury, Jupiter, and Mars are in Aries
Vesta and Pluto   are in Gemini
Neptune   is in Cancer
The Moon   is in Leo
Pallas, Ceres, and Uranus   are in Sagittarius
Chiron   is in Capricorn
Juno and Saturn   are in Aquarius
Venus   is in Pisces

The Sun, Mercury, Jupiter, and Mars are in Aries, which is ruled by Mars. Mars is the dispositor of those planets.

Vesta and Pluto are in Gemini, which is ruled by Mercury and Mercury is in Aries. Since Mars rules Aries, it is also the dispositor of Vesta and Pluto.

The Moon is in Leo, ruled by the Sun. The Sun is in Aries, ruled by Mars. So Mars is the ultimate dispositor of the Moon.

Pallas, Ceres and Uranus are in Sagittarius, ruled by Jupiter. Jupiter is in Aries, ruled by Mars. Mars is the ultimate dispositor of Pallas, Ceres, and Uranus.

Chiron is in Capricorn, ruled by Saturn. Saturn is in Aquarius, ruled by Uranus. Uranus is in Sagittarius, ruled by Jupiter. Jupiter is in Aries, ruled by Mars. Mars is the ultimate dispositor of Chiron.

Juno and Saturn are in Aquarius, ruled by Uranus. Uranus is in Sagittarius, ruled by Jupiter. Jupiter is in Aries, ruled by Mars. Mars is the dispositor of Juno and Saturn.

Venus is in Pisces, ruled by Neptune. Neptune is in Cancer, ruled by the Moon. The Moon is in Leo, ruled by the Sun. The Sun is in Aries, ruled Mars. Mars is the ultimate dispositor of Venus.

The above is an example of a *singleton* dispositor. One planet, Mars, is the ultimate ruler of all of the planets and the Sun and Moon. More often there will be two dispositors, or more. When planets are in the sign that they rule, no other planet may be their dispositor. If in this chart Saturn had been in his own sign, Capricorn, we would have had two dispositors.

In this chart, the planet Mars is a very significant principle. It must mean that pioneering leadership is a motivating factor in this person's life and that heroism, masculinity and courage are highly valued qualities.

Dissociate Signs. Adjacent signs—30 degrees apart—and signs which are separated by 150 degrees. Also called the semi-sextile and the inconjunct or quincunx. These signs have nothing in common with each other. They do not share the same Quadrature (Cardinal, Fixed, or Mutable) with each other, nor do they have in common the same Triplicity (Fire, Air, Earth, or Water). Different from each other in every respect they are the aspects that indicate the potential for adjustment and growth.

Diurnal: By day. Planets are diurnal when they are above the Horizon. Planets above the Horizon operate in circumstances that bring one out into the world and away from the private, inner side of life. Nocturnal planets do just the opposite. All of those circumstances concerning the houses from seven to twelve (those above the Horizon) will be more active and have

55

greater emphasis if they are occupied by planets. (see Houses)

Dog Star: Sirius, a star of the first magnitude, located in the constellation Canis Major. Its position corresponds with the 13th degree of Cancer. The Sun's conjunction with the star gave rise to the expression, "dog days of summer." If this star has any significance, I am not aware of it.

Double-bodied: A term applied to Mutable or Common signs. (see Mutable)

Dragon's Head; Dragon's Tail: The North and South Nodes. (see Caput Draconis)

Dumb Signs: Also called "mute." These are the signs Cancer, Scorpio, and Pisces; the reptilian signs. The creatures which represent them—the Crab, the Scorpion, and the Fish—make no audible sound. The inarticulate signs are Aries, Taurus, Leo, and Capricorn, as distinguished from the "articulate" or human signs, Gemini, Virgo, Libra, Sagittarius, and Aquarius. The fact that man and the lower orders of life have some characteristics in common may have struck the ancients and disposed them to select these creatures as symbols and apply them to the expression of human faculty and character.

Eagle: Mythologically, this bird is associated with Jupiter. (We should remember that it is a raptor, a predatory bird.) It is said that Jupiter, in the form of an eagle, abducted the beautiful youth Ganymedes and carried him to Olympus to become cup-bearer to the gods. Ganymedes' image was later set among the stars as Aquarius, the water-carrier.

Astrologically, it is often said that the eagle is associated with the sign Scorpio, as indication of soaring, transcending, and rising above the intense stresses to which Scorpio is subject. So is the Phoenix associated with Scorpio as symbolic of rebirth, rising again out of the ashes.

EARTH SIGNS: The Earth Triplicity includes the signs Capricorn, Taurus, and Virgo; one Cardinal, one Fixed, and one Mutable. They represent three aspects of the psychological function of sensation, which is to say they describe experience through the senses — what we can see, hear, touch, smell, and taste. These are perceptive signs, but they are not selective or preferential. They merely perceive and register reality regardless of whether it is pleasant or not. This helps to develp discrimination and taste.

The Earth signs are feminine signs, for they represent the feminine capacity to give form to things. The feminine, the woman, labors and produces the child. Mother Earth labors and produces things of the Earth; grain and fruit, plants and trees. The feminine element in *man or woman* is productive, realistic, practical, sensible, sensitive, loves to tinker with reality, and wants something to show for its effort. It is a materialistic element for it deals with matter.

These people may become manufacturers, builders, engineers. They have the ability to conceive, design, and structure. We find among these earthy people, architects, craftsmen, artisans. They are surveyors, map-makers. They know how to categorize, how to sort things out, how to solve problems realistically, and how to perceive what is really there. They are troubleshooters and crisis-handlers.

It is this element that is necessary for the artist, the critic, the connoisseur. It is responsible for the development of expertise and skill in handling tools and materials and for proficiency in the refinement of one or another of the senses: physical sensitivity, singing, dancing, surgery, safe-cracking, taste-testing, scent-testing, color-coordinating, painting sculpting, etc.

ECLIPSES: A New Moon is a conjunction of Sun and Moon. A solar eclipse is a special kind of New Moon and occurs when the Moon is on the Ecliptic and at the proper distance from Earth so that when the conjunction occurs, her disc will appear to be the exactly the same size as the Sun and will precisely cover it for several minutes, shutting off the light of the

Sun. When that happens we earthlings are treated to seeing the wonder of the Sun's corona glowing around the disc of the Moon, a very magical, awe-inspiring occurrence.

A Full Moon is an opposition between the two Lights. A lunar eclipse is a special kind of Full Moon and occurs when the Moon is once again on the Ecliptic, but now the Earth is between the Sun and Moon, and the Earth's shadow darkens the Moon.

The old time astrologers considered eclipses to be of evil portent, signifying catastrophe for mankind. And that may be the case, for even ordinary New and Full Moons literally do have a gravitational effect on the Earth, especially the waters and other Earth fluids—possibly even the inner fluid core of the earth—resulting in especially high tides and perhaps inner surges of magma. Thus there is often severe flooding and perhaps movement of the continental plates, resulting in earthquake. The parallel effect on humans and animals is excessive emotional responsiveness: there is an increased activity in hospital emergency rooms and local police precincts at the times of and just following New and especially Full Moons. How much more potent is the eclipse?

ECLIPTIC: The Ecliptic is the path of the Earth in its orbit about the Sun. But we transfer this Earth motion to the Sun and see it as the Sun's passage from sign to sign in its movement through the Zodiac. Because the Earth is inclined 23 degrees and 27 minutes on its axis, this path of the Sun's apparent journey is just that much inclined to the plane of the Earth's equator.

When the Moon is on the Ecliptic, there is opportunity

for a solar or lunar eclipse to occur, for the Moon may then pass in front of the Sun, or the Earth may pass between the Moon and Sun.

There may be planetary eclipses, too. When either Venus or Mercury is on the Ecliptic and passing in front of the Sun, we call those occasions Inferior Conjunctions, but Mercury and Venus will only appear as dark spots crossing the surface of the Sun. We can hardly call this an eclipse, but it is a very important Conjunction, the planetary equivalent of a solar eclipse. It doesn't happen very often; with Mercury it occurs about four times in 33 years, with Venus about four times in 243 years.

When any of the other planets are on the Ecliptic, and the earth is between them and the Sun, we call that an Opposition, the planetary equivalent of a lunar eclipse. When any of the planets are on the far side of the Sun and on the Ecliptic, we call it a Conjunction. The planet Uranus is always within a degree of the Ecliptic and is always in an eclipse relationship to the Sun.

Elections: The choice of a time to initiate work or enterprise of importance: beginning a journey, launching a vessel, starting a new business, moving to a new residence, signing a contract, getting married, etc. In my opinion, this is a terrible practice that many astrologers indulge in—playing God. It is presumptuous, foolhardy, and even dangerous. Life is far too complicated for mere humans to think they can outsmart God. Although many astrologers engage in this practice, its results are not easy to prove and may even be disastrous. If an enterprise initiated upon the advice of an astrologer who has determined its "proper" birth time turns out to be a success, credit will be given to the astrologer. If it fails, astrology itself is blamed. But how do we know that the enterprise wasn't successful simply because of its merit, or a failure because of its flaws? Neither evaluation is logical or useful: the first undermines our trust in our own planning and intuition, the second casts doubt on the validity of astrology.

Elevated: One of the accidental dignities. The highest point in the chart. A planet in the ninth or tenth houses, usually. A planet so elevated represents a principle to which one "looks up." Well, this is symbolically significant, so it probably does have some validity. Not much though.

Elongation: The distance of a planet from the Sun, whether east or west of it. Mercury cannot have an elongation greater than 28 degrees, and Venus no greater than 48 degrees. When east of the Sun and at their maximum elongation these planets will appear to slow down in order to turn Retrograde. The westward elongation is when the planet again slows down and prepares to start moving Direct.

EPHEMERIS or plural EPHEMERIDES: An almanac listing the daily noon or midnight positions of the Sun, Moon, and planets (as well as other astronomical phenomena) as seen from the observatory at Greenwich, England.

Equator: The great circle lying midway between the North and South Poles, dividing the Earth into two hemispheres, north and south. The Celestial Equator is an extension of this plane to the distant stars. (see Great Circle)

Equinox: There are two times in the year when the Sun crosses the Equator, making day and night of equal length in all parts of the Earth. The vernal equinox occurs about March 21st when the Sun enters Aries, the first day of spring; and the autumnal equinox occurs about September 22nd when the Sun enters Libra, the first day of fall. Of course these are the times when Ecliptic and Equator converge. It is said that the Earth is in such equilibrium at these times that one can easily balance an egg on its end.

Extroverted: See Jung.

Feeling: This is the psychological function associated with the Fire signs Aries, Leo, and Sagittarius. It is not necessarily emotional, unless carried to an extreme degree. It really has to do with the feeling values we place upon things and with appropriate functioning in accordance with the requirements of any specific situation. You wouldn't wear a bathing suit to a formal ball. Your feeling-judgement would tell you it is unsuitable. Nor would you offer your congratulations to the grieving widow at a funeral. A well-developed feeling function intervenes and the proper sentiment is expressed.

Feeling tells us our attitude about things, our likes and dislikes. And we act accordingly. Thus the childlike exuberance and anticipation felt by the Aries person when embarking on an adventure, the talent Leo has for projecting the appropriate vocal, facial, and physical qualities in a theatrical performance or just the flare for drama when it comes to a task as simple as wrapping a Christmas gift, and the shared enthusiasm and delight projected by Sagittarius.

FEMININE PLANETS: Until the asteroids became a part of the astrologer's palette the only truly feminine planets were the Moon and Venus. The Moon is ruler of the Water sign Cancer and Venus is the ruler of the Earth sign Taurus. But as you can see below, there are six feminine element signs and yet, the astrology we use has masculine principle planets ruling most of them. It is my belief that the assignation of masculine rulers to feminine signs is a consequence of the emergence of patriarchy in the Aries Age, the age in which the Great Mother and the feminine were generally degraded, devalued and displaced. Their realms were transferred to masculine deities. Thus Saturn became the ruler of the feminine Earth sign Capricorn, and also ruled the masculine Air sign Aquarius; Mercury was said to be the ruler not only of the masculine Air sign Gemini, but of the feminine Earth sign Virgo; Jupiter was in charge of both the masculine Fire sign Sagittarius and the feminine Water sign Pisces; Mars was the ruler of the masculine Fire sign Aries and the feminine Water sign Scorpio. Later, when the more recent planets were discovered, Neptune was given Pisces, Pluto was given Scorpio. Despite the fact that the asteriods were known, Mercury and Venus retained their dual rulerships.

It is my belief that all the feminine signs should be ruled by feminine principle planets and the masculine signs by masculine principle planets with the exception of Capricorn and Libra noted below.

FEMININE SIGNS AND PLANETS	MASCULINE SIGNS AND PLANETS
Taurus ruled by Venus	Aries ruled by Mars

Cancer ruled by Moon	Gemini ruled by Mercury
Virgo ruled by Ceres and Vesta	Leo ruled by Sun
Scorpio ruled by Pluto	*(Libra ruled by Juno and Pallas the most feminine of the masculine Signs)
*(Capricorn ruled by Saturn—the most masculine of the feminine Signs)	
	Sagittarius ruled by Jupiter
Pisces ruled by Neptune	Aquarius ruled by Uranus

It is not unreasonable to suppose that Pluto and Neptune are usurpers of the feminine realms of the sea and the underworld, that they are stand-ins for the more appropriate rulers of Pisces and Scorpio. Amphitrite was the goddess of the Sea, "la Mer," the mother from which all life has emerged. Persephone was Queen of the Underworld, who, according to Graves, represents the hope of rebirth in contrast with Pluto's harsher message of the ineluctability of death.

As for Saturn, the ruler of Capricorn, he is the stand-in for the great and ancient mountain goddess, she who wielded great power, and who must be obeyed. There is a certain strict practicality about this sign, a hardness, a no-nonsense outlook that may be considered somewhat masculine. And Libra, a masculine Air sign, has a softness, reasonableness, and cooperative potential that is suggestive of the feminine. It certainly bespeaks qualities which are the very antithesis of the message of Aries, the sign which is its opposite. Juno and Pallas are the best representatives of these qualities. As in the symbol for Yang-Yin, in the masculine side there is a touch of the feminine and in the feminine side there is a touch of the masculine.

FEMININE SIGNS: The three Earth signs Capricorn, Taurus, and Virgo, and the three Water signs Cancer, Scorpio, and Pisces. These are irrational-perceptive signs (and by irrational we do not mean unreasonable, but simply that these perceptions are non-judgmental; one does not have to think about them. If you bang your shin, it hurts, it is a given; if you have a hunch about something, it simply presents itself.) Earth is perceptive of reality (sensation) and water is perceptive of the intangible (intuition).

These are also called negative signs. They tend to be more passive-receptive; earth signs are receptive and responsive to sensual stimuli and water signs are receptive and responsive to psychic stimuli.

FIRE SIGNS: The Fire Triplicity, Aries, Leo, and Sagittarius. One Cardinal, one Fixed, and one Mutable. In astrology, the Fire signs represent three aspects of the psychological function feeling. As the great psychologist Jung points out, it is very difficult to describe precisely what we mean by feeling, for to do so we must use thinking—words and ideas—which is the opposite of feeling. Feeling is . . . feeling . . . wordless, thoughtless, felt inside, in the heart in Leo, in the dizzy headiness of Aries, and in the gonads of Sagittarius. And so in trying to explain what is meant by feeling we must resort to certain feeling-toned words which do convey some idea of what we mean, but mere words cannot induce the experience of the actual feeling itself: words such as enthusiasm, excitement, delight, bliss, pleasure, thrill, ardor, fervor, passion, zeal, zest, verve, aspi-

FEMININE SIGNS

EARTH   WATER

♉ ♍ ♑   ♋ ♏ ♓

SENSATION   INTUITION

IRRATIONAL-PERCEPTIVE

CONSCIOUS   UNCONSCIOUS

CONSCIOUS	UNCONSCIOUS
things	visions
physical	psychic
particular	universal
circumscribed	unlimited
exacting	permissive
skills	potentials
discriminating	solicitous
practicality	possibility
concrete	fluid
realistic	prophetic
sensible	emotional
structuring	nurturing
earth-bound	imaginative
sensual	mystical
reality	fantasy
substantial	vague
system	chance
esthetic	poetic
hardheaded	gullible
rigid	malleable
critical	compassionate
sober	intoxicated
careful	sloppy

ration, desire, will, and drama; and when negative, fear, disgust, horror, dread, revulsion, contempt, distaste, and displeasure. Feelings may be positive or negative, but they always express a value judgment, a like or a dislike, and this is what the Fire signs are all about. They are not necessarily emotional, but when feelings become extreme, they may manifest emotionally, with tears or laughter, or physically, with bodily innervations.

FIXED SIGNS: The Fixed signs are those that are found in the second month of each season: Taurus, Leo, Scorpio, and Aquarius. These signs have no touch with the Great Cardinal Cross which defines the solstices and equinoxes. They are sheltered from the turbulent activity and change that characterize those signs that fall on either side of that Great Cross. Consequently, there is a greater steadiness and calm to be found in these signs. A quiet that permits introspection, greater subjectivity, analysis, and search for meaning. Outer turbulence and crisis are not demanding attention. These signs are slower, unhurried, more phlegmatic, more plodding. Their actions are determined more by inner ideals, images, and values than by outer circumstances. These people are not so much concerned with today or yesterday as they are geared to the future, looking ahead not to tomorrow but to many days beyond tomorrow. They are farsighted. The general attitude type that they describe may be called introverted.

FIXED STARS: All of the bright, twinkly lights up there in the night sky that stay in the same constellations or groupings are stars, not planets. Planets are members of the solar system which move and have orbits that take them on their journeys around the Sun. Stars are not members of the solar system and are very far away. The closest star is Alpha Centauri and is about four and one half light years away from us.

Many astrologers believe that some stars, especially those of the brightest magnitude, have some kind of particular significance. If this were the case, we would be using these stars in our horoscopic analyses with great conviction, but we aren't.

This is a subject that needs much study.

FORM OF BODY: The physical appearance of the person. We are such a melding or blending of the various signs in which our planets are located that I have taken to describing the horoscope as being analogous to a recipe for a particular dish. The Ascendant would be the name of the dish, its identity (and may, for that reason, play the greatest role, but not the only one in determining the appearance of the person); the Sun and Moon would be the main ingredients that go into the recipe, the Sun representing the dry ingredients and the Moon the liquids; and the planets would be the flavorings and spices that give the dish its distinctive bouquet. Thus no single element would have exclusive significance, but the horoscope would be seen as a combination or blending of elements, the sum total of which would be the dish, or the individual. (see Anatomy)

Fortuna, or Pars Fortuna: (see Arabian Parts)

Fruitful Signs: These are said to be the Water signs Cancer, Scorpio, and Pisces. It is a literal fact that without water there can be no growth.

Galactic Center: The center of our galaxy around which the Sun revolves. Said to be in the area of 25 – 26 Sagittarius. It is not certain that there is any mysterious potency to any planets or points found in this vicinity of the Zodiac.

Galileo: (1565 – 1642) In 1609 a messenger from Venice brought Galileo the news that someone had constructed a spyglass that made distant objects appear to be close by. So Galileo set to work and constructed one of his own. Within weeks he made a series of discoveries that began a whole new era in astronomy. First he observed the Moon, and measured correctly the height of one of its mountains from the shadow it cast. Next he peered at the Milky Way and was probably the first human to see that it is composed of billions of stars. Then he discovered the four brightest moons of Jupiter, that Venus has phases, and he saw Saturn's rings, though not clearly enough to know what they really were. His was essentially a Copernican model of the universe.

GEMINI: Gemini is the Mutable sign in the Air Triplicity.

It is a double-bodied sign. Thus, although Gemini is an Air sign and therefore expresses a thinking function, it seems to borrow a measure of another function—intuition—from the sign Cancer, toward which it is heading. And so we say that the psychological function that Gemini manifests is a blend of thinking with intuition; it is a Thinking-Intuitive sign and the general attitude it projects may be called Centrovert since it is found between a fixed sign on one side—Taurus—and a Cardinal sign on the other—Cancer. Or it may be called Ambivert since it does have a dual function.

Gemini is the third month of the spring season, a time of the year when people are spending a lot of time outdoors chatting over the backyard fence with neighbors, going for walks in the spring air, having block parties in cities, shopping in open air flea-markets, driving around in their cars, enjoying the new green and the flowery blooms of spring, and anticipating summer vacations. It is the month of roses.

Obviously this sign, whose ruler is Mercury, the godling who is said to have invented the alphabet, is a very perceptive and communicative sign. The great drive in Gemini is to share perceptions with others, to listen to and to tell stories. Geminians are "people persons" for they need people with whom to share their perceptions. Words and language are most important in Gemini. In fact, there is often talent with linguistics when planets are found in this sign. Letter-writers and postal workers are comfortable with Gemini, as is anyone involved with communications.

This is the sign that is associated with the news media and journalists (messengers), where the questions who, what, where, when, why, and how are asked. Indeed, Gemini is the most curious and questioning of the signs. We often say a good newspaper person has "a nose for news." This is where intuition comes in with this sign. The nose is symbolic of intuition; "I smell a rat." "Something is rotten in Denmark." Geminians have a knack for asking the right question to get the information that they suspect may be there, or they may magically seem to be in the right place at the right time to scoop the story.

This is the sign whose Zodiac symbol is "The Twins," and planets here often denote the existence of siblings, or imply that siblings may be very significant in one's life. This sign has much in common with the third house which is the house of communication, and close relatives such as siblings and cousins are found here, as are neighbors. Cars and short journeys are also in the sphere of Gemini and the third house. People with an emphasis on Gemini are often very busy with typewriters, word processors, telephones, and/or the more recent developments in high-tech communication.

Occasionally one hears the expression "dual personality" or "split personality" applied to this sign, and that is really very unfair. These terms describing psychological pathology may be applied to any sign of the Zodiac. What is true of Gemini is the ability to do more than one thing at a time, and a talent for versatility.

Gems: Gems and minerals have always been associated with the signs of the Zodiac. The list below names one or two stones that are usually connected with each sign. There are other sign allocations for these, and many other stones.

Aries	— diamond, bloodstone
Taurus	— emerald, rose quartz
Gemini	— agate, turquoise
Cancer	— pearl, moonstone
Leo	— citrine, topaz
Virgo	— lapis, amazonite
Libra	— opal, sapphire
Scorpio	— smoky quartz, ruby
Sagittarius	— azurite, carbuncle
Capricorn	— garnet, peridot
Aquarius	— aquamarine
Pisces	— amethyst, chrysolite

General Attitude: (see Jung)

Geniture: Birth.

Geocentric: Having the Earth for a center. Astrology is Earth-centered. How could it be otherwise? Here we are on the Earth. Our view of the Zodiac is from the Earth. What the signs and planets signify must be from an Earth-centered perspective. It would be arrogant of us to presume that the Earth conditioned meanings of the signs and planets would have the same relevance from the perspective of any other body in the solar system, including the Sun. The Zodiac as we know it does not exist on the Sun or on any other planet; the significance of the signs of the zodiac has been projected onto the heavens from the Earth, and that significance stems from the conditions on the Earth in each season, and not vice versa. It is the Earth's inclination on its axis that creates the seasons and therefore the signs.

GLYPHS:

SIGNS

Aries ♈   Libra ♎
Taurus ♉   Scorpio ♏
Gemini ♊   Sagittarius ♐
Cancer ♋   Capricorn ♑
Leo ♌   Aquarius ♒
Virgo ♍   Pisces ♓
Dragon's Head ☊   Tail ☋

PLANETS

Sun ☉   Jupiter ♃
Moon ☽   Saturn ♄
Mercury ☿   Uranus ♅
Venus ♀   Neptune ♆
Mars ♂   Pluto ♇
Ceres ⚳   Vesta ⚶
Pallas ⚴   Juno ⚵

Grand Trine: (see Aspects)

The Greater Benefic: The planet Jupiter is called the Greater Benefic. This medieval title encourages astrologers to want to see nothing but great good fortune with aspects to or from Jupiter or with what is thought to be favorable placement of this planet. This certainly is the biggest planet, and often the brightest. It is a planet of excesses, of expansion; we know enough in our time to realize that too much, even of a good thing, is very often not a desirable condition at all. (see Jupiter)

Gregorian Calendar: On October 5th, 1582, Pope Gregory decreed that this date should be changed to October 15th. This changed the old calendar, called the Julian Calendar, to the new calendar, the Gregorian. However, the old-style calendar, the Julian, persisted for centuries after this date in various places, to this day giving astrologers a big headache.

Heliocentric Astrology: Sun centered astrology. Hard to fathom for as viewed from the Sun the Zodiac does not exist. The Zodiac is created by the Earth, by the Earth's inclination on its axis, which creates the seasons and thus the three months of each season and thus the 12 signs. From the perspective of the Sun or any other planet the Zodiac as we know it does not exist. And yet there are many astrologers who practice heliocentric astrology and are convinced of its validity.

Heliocentric Longitude and Latitude: The Nautical Almanac gives the heliocentric positions of all celestial bodies, but in terms of the 360 degrees of the circle. The astrologer's ephemerides are a conversion of these heliocentric positions to their geocentric equivalent, that is, to their location in the Tropical Zodiac from an Earth-centered perspective.

Hexagon: Six sextiles. A Grand Sextile. (see Configurations)

HIDDEN ASPECTS: A mutual aspect made by a transiting planet to a degree sensitized by the nature of a planet that had a station at this point and continued to move on. This responsiveness or sensitivity can endure for a long time, as much as two years in the case of Mars. It is called a Hidden Aspect to differentiate it from a normal or overt aspect wherein both degrees are actually occupied by a transiting planet. (see Sensitive Degrees)

Horary Astrology: A system of astrological practice in which a horoscope is created for the time a question is asked of the astrologer. It is a system of prognostication similar to the *I Ching,* based on the idea that the moment contains an image of the situation—the direction in which the situation is inclined—and therefore the answer to the question, whatever it may be. "The Moment" in this context is the moment the astrologer understands the question. The horoscope is set up for that moment, and the consequent configuration yields information which the astrologer interprets. With regard to the *I Ching,* "the Moment" occurs at the tossing of coins or yarrow stalks, and the consequent hexagrams which contain relevant information are interpreted by the student of the *I Ching.*

There are certain rules for reading these charts which serve to eliminate frivolous questions or impossible situations. These horoscopes have as much validity as the *I Ching,* Tarot Cards, reading tea leaves or coffee grounds, animal entrails, tortoise shells, pebbles bouncing in a basin of water, or any other prognosticating device you can think of. Undoubtedly a high measure of psychic ability is required to successfully interpret them.

Horizon: A great circle intersecting the Ecliptic which appears in a horoscope as a horizontal line marking the points of the Ascendant and Descendant. (see Circles)

Horoscope: The birth map or chart. A diagram showing the positions of the planets in the signs and houses, which they occupy at the time and place of birth.

HOUSES OF THE HOROSCOPE: A house in the astronomical sense is one twelfth of the prime vertical. This latter is the circle in which one stands upright when facing due south. As the Zodiac does not lie in the same plane with this prime vertical, the signs of the Zodiac pass through the houses obliquely, and for the same reason the planets pass through them at angles varying according to their several declinations. In extreme northern latitudes it is possible to have more than one sign in the same house.

The houses define the various spheres of human activity, the circumstances of life. Planets located in these houses show where and what the action is in one's life. The sign on the cusp of the house tells the mode of manifestation of those circumstances that the house describes.

First House: the Ascendant

The conscious standpoint, the ego, or that aspect of self which is most readily at hand in any immediate situation.

Those matters that are taken personally by the individual.

The physical body to a certain extent.

The talents, gifts, and faults indicated by the Rising Sign.

Second House:

Possessions, assets, or whatever the person has that is of value or through which money can be generated.

Moveable goods or liquid assets.

Values, sometimes intangible moral, or ethical—such as integrity.

Money as liberty and freedom to act.

Third House:

Communication, conversation, writing.

Siblings and blood relatives, except parents and children.

Neighbors, local parochial environment.

Short journeys, mass transit, including cars, trains, and other vehicles of transport. Local coming and going. Roads and highways.

Conveniences we take-for-granted; telephones, typewriters, computers.

Fourth House: (The cusp of the fourth House is called the Imum Coeli, or the Nadir)

Home, soul, safety, rest, privacy.

Foundations in general.

Family honor, background, and tradition; roots in the clan or race.

Inheritance; realty owned or used.

Father as that parent who provides basic security.

Fifth House:

Pleasure, simple self-expression, self-discovery, creativity.

Children, projections of self.

Lovers.

Personal discipline, schools, the process of learning.

Prodigality, dissipation, gambling, speculation.

Amusements, entertainment, theatre, fun and games, hobbies, toys.

Sixth House:

Work, service, servants, co-workers.

Labor, productivity, work routines.

Sickness and health, the care one gives oneself, therapeutic activity.

Malcontent, work as drudgery.

Pets and small animals.

Magic.

Aunts and uncles.

Seventh House:

This is the cusp of the Descendant, the western Horizon where planets set.

An old name for this house was "the house of open enemies." It is the house of marriage.

Partnership of every sort, cooperation with others, tête-à-tête relationships, direct competition in friendship, or enmity.

Lawyers and legal action; professional consultation.

Fine arts, extraordinary achievement.

Buying and selling.

Eighth House:

Death, rebirth, transformation and transcendence.

The willingness or necessity to "let go," to yield, to put oneself in another's hands. Sex and death require such an attitude or capacity and thus may also contain the potential for rebirth or rejuvenation; new cycles.

Being limited by another's ideas or values.

The talents and resources of others.

The partner's money or resources.

Indebtedness, or, on the other hand, moneys owed.

Frozen resources and trust funds.

Wills, legacies, minor inheritances.

Possession by other entities.

Ninth House:

The house of travel and contact with foreigners.

Higher consciousness, expanded knowledge, higher learning (university level).

Inspiration, visions, vicarious living.

Moral and ethical consciousness.

Court procedures, legal practice.

Publishing, lecturing, broadcasting; fame (notoriety, being known abroad).

Tenth House:

This is the Zenith of the chart, the Midheaven, the Medium Coeli or MC. Planets in the ninth and tenth houses are said to be elevated.

The figure one cuts in the world, public image, persona. (Not necessarily fame).

Profession, disciplined capacities.

The initial authority figure in one's life, a parent—usually the mother.

One's employer, or boss.

Active heads of any enterprise.

Administrators of property, landlords, proprietors.

Eleventh House:

Friends, acquaintances, casual ties with others.

Friendly help given and/or received.

Companies, organizations, groups, clubs.

Hopes and wishes, goals and intentions, one's life path.

Public relations, promotional activities.

Idealized projects. Social consciousness.

Twelfth House:

Institutionalization of life; prisons, hospitals.

Escape from bondage, reprieves, pardons.

Secret sorrows, secret joys. Psychological support as well as restriction.

Research, detection, investigation, background planning and preparation, writing relative to career.

Spiritual resources, unexpressed devotion, unsuspected help, subconscious guidance.

The astrologers of the Dark Ages called this "the house of hidden enemies."

HOUSE CATEGORIES: *Angular Houses* These are the four houses adjacent to and located on the counter-clockwise side of the 90 degree angles formed by the intersection of the Horizon and the Meridian, the Cardinal Cross: the first and seventh, fourth and tenth houses. These opposing houses deal with fundamental circumstances of life. The first house is concerned with self, the seventh with not-self, or partner, and the potential for opportunity. The fourth house represents home and security, the tenth position in the world. These houses are involved with the immediate present.

Succedent Houses: Moving counter-clockwise, these are the houses following the angular houses. They do not touch the Cardinal Cross. The second and eighth, fifth, and eleventh houses. The second house influences the expression of personal values and the eighth influences the recognition of or

HOUSES

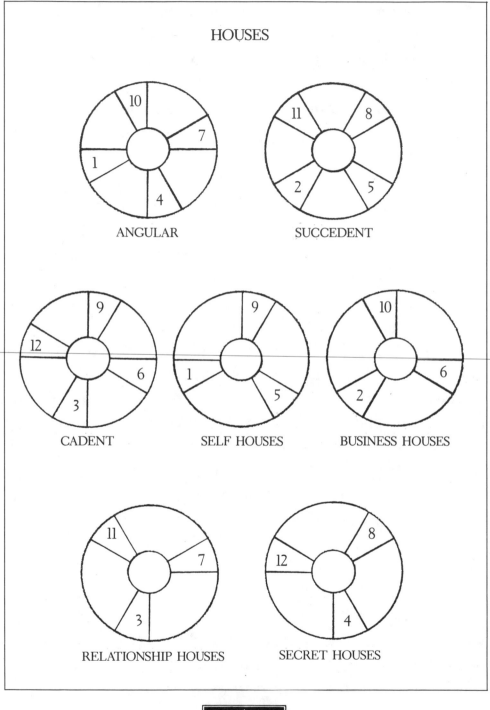

ANGULAR

SUCCEDENT

CADENT

SELF HOUSES

BUSINESS HOUSES

RELATIONSHIP HOUSES

SECRET HOUSES

limitation by the values of others. Both are concerned with money as a symbol of value. The fifth house is concerned with self-expression and self-projection, the eleventh with the need to share these with and be part of a community. All of these houses are geared to the fulfillment of potential; future oriented.

Cadent Houses: Closing the triad, these houses complete the connection with the Cardinal Cross but on the clockwise side. The third and ninth, sixth and twelfth houses. The first pair of houses have an outward impulse, the second pair an inward impulse. The third house represents personal involvement with the immediate environment, neighbors, and near relatives. The ninth expresses the need for the personal transcendence of these parochial limitations through learning and travel. The sixth house is the need to give attention to and take responsibility for personal well being in connection with both work and personal care, health. The eleventh house is the need to submit to outwardly imposed routine and regimen as well as self imposed discipline or preparation in the pursuit of some endeavor. These houses are concerned with the past or with background elements.

There is another way of categorizing the houses:

The Self Houses: first—identity, fifth—projection of self (off-spring), and ninth—self-transcendence (knowledge).

The Relationship Houses: third—siblings and environment, seventh—partnership and opportunity, and 11th—friendship and self-promotion.

The Houses of Concern: second—possessions and resources, sixth—duty, work and self-care, and tenth—profession, honor and the figure you cut in the world.

The Houses of Privacy, the Secret Houses: fourth—home and privacy, eighth—regeneration, and twelfth—confinement, self-imposed or otherwise, and research.

House Systems: The signs are 30 degree segments of the circle of the Ecliptic. But the houses are a twelve-fold division of one or another Prime Meridian which identifies the circumstances of life as described briefly above, with the first house always just below the Horizon in the east. There are many systems for creating this twelve-fold division of circumstances, the most popular being the Placidus system in the U.S.; there is also the Campanus system, popular in Europe, the Koch system, the Regiomontanous, the Morinus, and an Equal House system, which assigns 30 degrees to each and every house (which is not the case with the other systems), etc. To understand the rationale for the different systems of house division you must find an astrologer who has made a study of all of them. I have not.

Human Signs: These are the signs whose symbols have human form: Gemini—the Twins; Virgo—the Virgin holding the sheaf of wheat; Libra—Justice holding the scales; Sagittarius—the centaur, part human, part animal; and Aquarius—the water bearer, the human figure pouring fertilizing waters upon the earth.

Hyleg: Or the Alpheta; Giver of Life. A complex system proposed by Ptolemy to identify places or planets in the horoscope that are conducive to life. Its opposite is the Anareta or Destroyer of Life. Most astrologers ignore it for in all of these centuries it is a theory which has not proven valid.

84

Imum Coeli: The bottom of the chart, the Nadir, the point directly under the Earth. The I.C. (see Houses)

Inconjunct: (see Aspects)

Inferior Planets: This refers to Mercury and Venus, both of which have orbits that are between Earth and Sun. Those planets that are outside the Earth's orbit are called "superior planets." This is not a values call; it is simply a differentiation.

Ingress: The entry of a planet into a sign and/or into a house.

Initiating Signs: (see the Cardinal Signs)

Inspirational Natures: (see Fire Signs)

Intellectual Natures: (see Air Signs)

Intercepted Signs: When the view of the Ecliptic from Earth is so oblique that there is a compression or foreshortening of certain signs and an expansion or spreading out of others, it will appear that one house (and its opposite) will contain more than one sign, i.e., a whole sign will be contained with no touch of that sign at either cusp. When that happens we say the sign is intercepted. As a consequence, there will be two adjacent

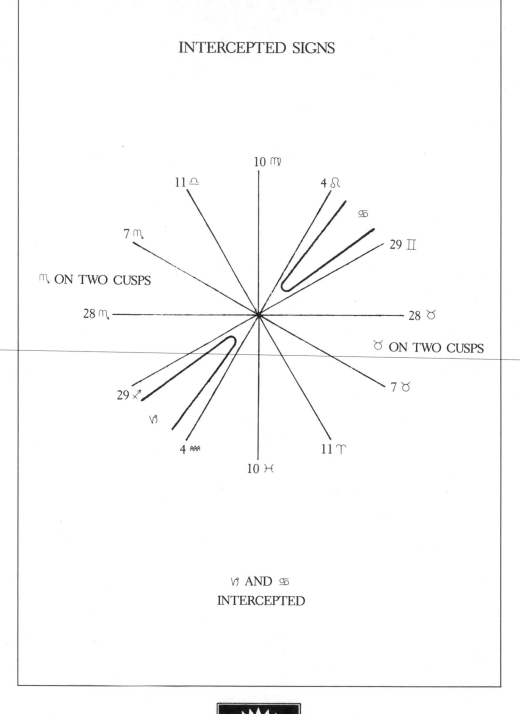

INTERCEPTED SIGNS

10 ♍

11 ♎

4 ♌

♋

29 ♊

7 ♏

♏ ON TWO CUSPS

28 ♏

28 ♉

♉ ON TWO CUSPS

29 ♐

7 ♉

♑

11 ♈

4 ♒

10 ♓

♑ AND ♋
INTERCEPTED

houses (and their opposites) having the same sign on their cusps. Since every sign is said to be ruled by a planet, the sign on the cusp of a house also tells us which planet is the ruler of the circumstances that the house describes. The sign on the cusp has primary significance. Thus when a sign is intercepted, the ruler of that sign does not have as great a power over the circumstances of the house that the intercepted sign is in as does the planet that rules the sign on the cusp.

Interpolation: Since the planets' positions are given only once a day at either noon or midnight relative to the observatory at Greenwich, England, an adjustment must be made to get the precise positions of the planets in other places at other times. Similarly, the house cusps must be adjusted for time and place. This adjustment is called interpolation.

Introversion: (see Jung)

INTUITION: This is the psychological function associated with the Water signs Cancer, Scorpio, and Pisces. Intuition is a perceptive function, but it is perception through no apparent means: knowing without knowing how one knows. We call it sympathy, empathy, sometimes compassion and these are qualities that are associated with these signs.

Cancer is best at sensing potential or possibilities. Pisces has the capacity to feel what may be happening to others as though it were happening to self, thus the compassion and empathy. Scorpio is more inclined to probe deeply into more dangerous or forbidden areas, seeking to unmask or expose hidden motives, and to get behind disarming, ingratiating facades.

Ishtar: As Venus was called in the ancient civilizations of the Middle East.

JONES, MARC EDMUND: Until his death in 1981, in his 90th year, Marc Edmund Jones was known as the "Dean" of American astrologers. In his book, *Astrology, How and Why it Works,* he defined the nature of the signs of the Zodiac: the Triplicities of elements—Fire, Air, Earth and Water—which he identifies as "functions," and the Quadratures—Cardinal, Fixed and Mutable—which he identifies as "temperament." Marc Jones had an intellect that was extremely analytical and penetrating. Though his style of writing was somewhat difficult, patience and study of his work yield insights into the factors of astrological analysis that are far more profound and relevant than so much of the superficial, often inaccurate though extremely entertaining and titillating output we are so familiar with.

It was his work that permitted the connection between the Signs of the Zodiac and the Psychological types of Jung to be so clearly perceived.

JUNG, CARL GUSTAV: It is the belief of this compiler that the psychological types described by C. G. Jung in his great work, *Psychological Types,* are the very same types identified by the signs of the Zodiac.

Jung proposes two general attitude types which he calls Introvert and Extrovert, and four psychological functions: Thinking, Feeling, Sensation and Intuition, which may manifest in either an introverted or an extroverted manner. There is a third general attitude proposed by Erich Neumann, a disciple of Jung, which he calls Centrovert. I believe this presents us with a third group of four functions which manifest in a Centroverted manner—neither introverted (subjective), nor extroverted (objective), but perhaps a little of both and also more interpersonal, and personality conscious, thus giving us the 12 types we need to conform to the 12 signs of the Zodiac. Actually, Jung himself was aware of the third group in the Centrovert category, for in the definitions section of *Psychological Types* Jung does describe a kind of blending of two functions in certain individuals, which is what happens with the Centrovert group. He describes a Thinking-Intuitive type, a Sensation-Thinking type, a Feeling-Sensation type and an Intuitive-Feeling type. It so happens that these dual-function types are perfectly in accord with the four Common or Mutable signs also called double-bodied; Gemini represents the Thinking-Intuitive type (he has a nose for news), Virgo representing the Sensation-Thinking type (putting the world in order), Sagittarius representing the Feeling-Sensation type (the sportsman, the businessman—facilitating administrator), and Pisces manifesting as the Intuitive-Feeling type (losing the self in love). Yes, Jung was aware of them, but apparently he did not recognize these combined functions as a third per-

CARDINAL
EXTRAVERTED

FEELING   ♈ ARIES

THINKING   ♎ LIBRA

SENSATION   ♑ CAPRICORN

INTUITION   ♋ CANCER

Energy and interest directed outward to objective experience. Captivated by immediate crises and events.

FIXED
INTROVERTED

FEELING   ♌ LEO

THINKING   ♒ AQUARIUS

SENSATION   ♉ TAURUS

INTUITION   ♏ SCORPIO

Motivation comes from within. Goal directed, idealizing. Subjective experience paramount. Abstracting. Inner ideals and values.

MUTABLE
CENTROVERTED

FEELING-SENSATION   ♐ SAGITTARIUS

THINKING-INTUITION   ♊ GEMINI

SENSATION-THINKING   ♍ VIRGO

INTUITION-FEELING   ♓ PISCES

Personal. Drawing upon inner AND outer experience. Personality building, building into self. Sharing, versatile, adaptable.

fectly valid group, and one which was neither introverted nor extroverted but perhaps shuttling between both modes as circumstances required and certainly with greater emphasis on personal relationships. We call those identified by the Mutable Signs "people persons."

It is my contention that the four Cardinal signs manifest in an Extroverted mode, the four Fixed signs manifest in an Introverted manner and the four Mutable signs manifest in a dual or Centroverted mode. And further that the four Elements are the four Functions, Air—Thinking, Fire—Feeling, Earth—Sensation, and Water—Intuition.

JUNO: Juno was the third asteroid to be discovered, on September 1, 1804. She is the smallest of the four classic asteroids. But does she ever pack a wallop! Juno has the most eccentric orbit of all the planets. This eccentricity brings her closer to the orbit of Mars than any of the other classic asteroids; she is close to Jupiter, too, but the orbit of Pallas is even closer. This is interesting. In mythology, Juno is the mother of Mars and the wife of Jupiter and Pallas is Jupiter's daughter. Juno's period of orbit is less than four and one-half years and she rotates in slightly more than seven hours.

Juno and Jupiter are the King and Queen of Heaven. Astronomically, they are quite a pair—Jupiter is the largest of the planets and Juno the smallest. But how very appropriate, in fact, is this discrepancy in size. It symbolizes the nature of their significance. Jupiter's massiveness is symbolic of his power and clout, and Juno's smallness represents that Queen of Heaven or no, she is the indicator of *powerlessness*. A large body in space has a very significant gravitational effect on other bodies, while

91

a small body has none.

Though Juno was the Queen of Heaven, she had no power, except, to some degree, the power to confer the gift of prophecy on humans or animals. It is said that the winds obeyed her. She has dominion over all matters that are important to women, especially relationship and childbirth.

Jupiter was a great philanderer, spreading his seed all over, impregnating nymphs and goddesses and mortal maidens, begetting other gods through them, and even bringing Ganymedes, the beautiful youth, to Olympus to replace Hebe as cup-bearer to the gods (which was taken by Plato to indicate celestial sanction of homosexual love). Further, Juno was an abused wife; more than once did Jupiter toss a thunderbolt at her and knock her about. Once, when all the gods had wearied of Jupiter's petulance and overbearing behavior, they attempted a coup, which failed. Jupiter, blaming Juno as the ringleader, punished her by hanging her from the heavens on golden chains around her wrists, with anvils attached to her ankles. (In those days slaves were punished in that fashion.) The Greeks portrayed Juno as a hellion: a jealous, mean, vindictive, and nagging wife. They could not imagine her to be anything else, having once given her such a charming, overbearing, abusive partner.

But Juno existed long before the Greeks had her seduced by Jupiter. She had been a great and revered goddess in the pre-Aries Age. She only became a powerless and abused wife when the Aries Age Greeks instituted marriage, bound her to Jupiter, and proclaimed the supremacy of Patriarchy over the Great Mother. This meant a loss of status for women in general,

92

for then marriage meant that they were completely subjugated by their husbands. And in the event of widowhood or spinsterhood, they were then under the power of their fathers, brothers, or uncles. Patriarchy did terrible things to women, stripping them of their dignity and of any control over their lives. They became mere chattel, stay-at-home drudges and childbearing machines.

But the Greek view of this aspect of the Great Goddess is too limited, for they have not considered all of the ramifications of the absence of the *desire for power*. When one has no need for power, there is no sense of the need to "lord" it over others. This opens the door to equal partnership. Juno is without power and that powerlessness is symbolic of the powerlessness that everyone experiences at one time or another, but especially women, children, minors, minorities, and the underprivileged, handicapped, and vanquished in battle.

What is the fruit of powerlessness? How do we cope with it? What must we do to survive when we are in a situation or position over which we have no control? We must learn how to deflect aggressive energy away from us, learn how to appease, to ingratiate, to tame, to disarm, to charm that power which could overwhelm us. Yes, indeed, Juno is a charmer. Venus arouses desire, but Juno charms.

How does she charm? In so many ways. For one thing she charms by enhancing the quality of life. She is an atmospheric, environmental principle. She creates a pleasant environment; she puts flowers on the table, lights candles, hangs curtains on the windows; she dresses beautifully (fashion is atmosphere and environment, too). She is a gracious hostess. This atmosphere-creating principle is absolutely essential at all parties and celebrations. She decks the halls . . . (Venus will pay the caterer, buy the clothes, engage the decorator; Juno *does* what Venus pays for).

Juno is the weaponless hand held out in friendship. Juno is civilized behavior, consideration for the vulnerability of others. Juno is manners and social finesse. She is the mother who says "Play nice, and don't fight." She teaches the child to share his toys. Juno is a gentling, humanizing, civilizing principle. She charms by being understanding. She is a relationship principle who knows how to give her interest and attention to "the other." She understands how other people feel. There is nothing more charming than that quality. It is most seductive. It is here we see her connection with Libra, the sign of relationship.

Juno is the capacity to mediate, to conciliate, to cooperate. Without that ability there can be no relationship, and in larger scope, no cooperation between peoples, no resolution of conflict. There would instead be war and barbarism. Juno is always active in diplomacy; she wants to avoid war at all costs, for there is nothing more destructive of the quality of life than war. Juno charms by being unthreatening, she has no weapons, she comes in peace. Because she is powerless, peace is essential for her survival and for the survival of her children. In war, Juno is the inevitable victim.

If it is true that it is the duty of the feminine to discipline the energies of the masculine, then that is the work of Juno. But we do not speak of woman only. We are speaking of that quality in both women and men that wants peace, civility, and cooperation rather than macho male aggressiveness, ever ready to resort to fighting, killing, and war to vanquish and subdue "the enemy."

But when things do not go well, then Juno can take two terrible and opposite forms other than those described above: she can manifest as a crass collaborator—a shameless sellout to the powers that be—a kind of "Stepford wife," totally fulfilling the male fantasy of the submissive woman or the happy slave, willing to be kept in slavery to save her own skin. Or she can become the Holy Terror, as the Greeks saw her, that is to say, a terrorist. Terrorism is the weapon of the powerless, and the terrible anger and outrage at powerlessness that is part of the Juno experience can lead to outrageous violations. It is not pretty. The abused child grows up to become a child abuser, the man who feels powerless within himself becomes the rapist or wife beater, powerless countries resort to training terrorists. Juno is the mother of Mars. Is this to say powerlessness breeds rage? I think so.

When is Juno outraged? When her charms and efforts at cooperation do not work, when there is rape, wife beating, child abuse, when the powerless are victimized, when minorities are given no hearing, when small countries are overrun by their larger neighbors, when might makes right, when all avenues to justice are closed, when diplomacy fails, when the powers that be will not listen to the grievances of the powerless, when there is injustice—then her only weapon is terrorism, the weapon of the powerless. Then there is hijacking, kidnapping, hostage-taking where the innocent become victims, the violated become violators.

Juno is a stormy goddess; the winds obey her. Violent storms, hurricanes, and tornadoes are symbolic of her rage, her outrage at powerlessness. Juno is the astrological indicator of violent storms as well as beautiful, balmy, pleasant weather. Juno is involved in all natural phenomena that affect the atmosphere. Juno is a meteorologist.

JUPITER: Jupiter is the largest of the planets. All the other planets combined would fit into Jupiter *one and one half times*. Jupiter has his own solar system of sorts—a big family of 16 satellites. The one called Ganymedes is as big as Mercury. Jupiter is an "almost star"—a potential star whose nuclear furnace never lighted. Had he been a little bit bigger, then Pouf! Nuclear incandescence! We just missed out on being a double-star system.

It is a fact that larger bodies in space have a gravitational impact on smaller ones. Bigness is symbolic of power and this giant planet affects the orbits not only of his own satellites and personal asteroids, the Trojans, but especially the asteroids of the Asteroid Belt, and, to some extent, all of the other comets and planets in the solar system.

Jupiter "throws his weight around." We speak of powerful people or countries as being able to do just that. They, too, affect the "orbits" of smaller bodies, or less powerful people. The point is, this physical fact of bigness regarding the planet Jupiter is a fitting symbol to describe the activity and principle that he represents: as The Boss, the director, the manager, the administrator; a person or corporation that impacts on others, whose actions and decisions profoundly affect the lives and circumstances of others with less power. This is the planet of Big Business. This is a power planet. And Jupiter's heavenly consort, little Juno, is the smallest of the bodies currently used in astrology, and represents—what else? Powerlessness. (It is important to avert the impression or to forestall coming to the conclusion that because Jupiter is big and has gravitational impact on other planets, that therefore aspects involving him are more important than those of any other planet or asteroid. Not so. Any other planet is doing *its* thing, and its thing is equally important. Jupiter just happens to be the planet that indicates bigness, influence, and administration, but this is no more significant than that which Juno represents—smallness and powerlessness).

An incredibly big body, Jupiter rotates on his axis in under 10 hours! I believe this symbolizes the busy activity of this principle and the sign he rules. We might say that Jupiter gets as much done in ten hours as we do in 24.

Another thing: Jupiter generates more energy than he receives from the Sun! This heat may be a consequence of his rapid rotation and the gravitational pressures of his great mass. Well, we all know that activity generates heat, and the release or spending of energy. Now, Jupiter is not only the manager, administrator, and businessman; he is the sportsman and ruler of the fall Fire Sign Sagittarius. There is no sport where energy is not generated and released. Even with board games people are apt to become pretty hot under the collar. The sign Sagittarius, though it appears in a cold month, is a Fire sign, and we all know that one of the ways of warming up in chilly weather is through movement, activity, sports. Children can work up a sweat with a winter snowball fight, for instance. Hunting, walking, running, and winter sports such as skiing and ice-skating are all activities that expend energy and generate heat.

Jupiter is an expanded body; he has enormous internal heat, and heat causes expansion. Astrologers have referred to Jupiter as the principle of expansion long before this astronomical fact about Jupiter was known. This expansiveness in Jupiterians manifests psychologically as enthusiasm and spontaneity (often excessive, manic), and physically as weight. The body expands, too. Jupiter and Sagittarius rule the legs, the thighs, and the fleshy part of the body. This inclination to heaviness could be the wise storing of potential fuel (fire) for the time of scarcity (like the bear) and/or to sustain surges of activity and movement.

The excessiveness of Jupiter can really be a problem. Jupiter is the manic side of the manic-depressive axis. There can be problems with biting off more than one can chew, over-expanding in some businesses, with inflation, exaggeration. With too-muchness. Bigger is not always better; sometimes less is more. The appellation "Greater Benefic" applied to Jupiter is not to be taken too literally.

Jupiter rules the legs and thighs. In ancient days, the main method of travel was walking, and, later, by horseback (the horse is associated with Sagittarius). So Jupiter has to do with the big walk, the big journey—travel. Now travel expands knowledge. Through travel we escape our local, parochial, all-too-familiar environment and head for strange, exotic places. Naturally, the thing to do when you have traveled and gained some knowledge is to "spread the word;" you lecture, write a book, you share your knowledge and experience with others. So Jupiter and the sign Sagittarius have to do with publishing, broadcasting, education, and higher learning. Knowledge of distant places and cultures results in a more philosophical perspective on life.

Jupiter is the most upright of the planets, for his equator is inclined to the ecliptic by only three degrees. "Upright," "upstanding," "standing tall." Physical facts have symbolic significance and I wouldn't be surprised if this fact about Jupiter symbolizes the kind of finger-wagging righteousness often found when either Jupiter or the sign he rules is prominent. Three degrees is a very slight axial tilt and it means that the seasons on Jupiter are negligible. They are just layered in bands north and south of his equator with very little change. The seasons are all going on at once, but stay put, in their latitudes, in their places, and do not change much with time. It does suggest a sort of rigidity, inflexibility, control. Things have to remain in place. His orbit (his year) takes almost 12 of our years.

This planet must be a very noisy place. The metal of Jupiter is tin, and it is said that there is nothing noisier than a tin drum. But the reason for the noisiness on Jupiter must be due to the enormous, violent, long-lasting storms — electrical storms, — thunderstorms which show up as swirling spots and colorful striped bands on his surface. Jupiter is bombastic.

Jupiter is called the Striped Giant, and silly as it seems, I have noticed that Jupiterian and Sagittarian types seem to like stripes. Consider the businessman's striped suit, for example, or the flashier stripes and checks of the sportsman and the racetrack tout.

Kepler, Johannes: Born in Germany and lived from 1571 – 1630. He was gifted in mathematics. Became an assistant to Tycho Brahe, who set him to work to try to find a satisfactory theory of planetary motion. He was an astrologer as well as a genius astronomer and his fame today rests primarily on his three laws of planetary motion, without which we would still be in the Dark Ages.

Key Words for the Planets:

Sun	Self, Purpose
Moon	Emotional response
Mercury	Consciousness
Venus	Gratification
Mars	Action
Jupiter	Administration
Saturn	Discrimination
Uranus	Individuality
Neptune	Conformity
Pluto	Obsession

Keywords for the Asteroids: Facets of the Feminine

Ceres	Mother	Food
Pallas	Daughter	Ingenuity
Juno	Wife	Clothing
Vesta	Sister	Shelter

Latitude: Angular distance north or south of a plane of the Ecliptic.

LEO: The sign Leo is the fifth sign of the Zodiac. It is the sign that arrives in the heart of summer when the Sun is at his maximum strength. The Sun is the ruler of the sign Leo. The Sun is the source of all life on Earth, but at this time of the year it can be scorching and overbearing, withering whatever it turns its gaze upon, and ever and always dimming the lights of even the brightest stars in the daytime sky. Overwhelming all others, Leo is "The Star."

Leo is the Fixed sign in the Fire Triplicity As a Fire sign, Leo expresses the psychological function feeling, but since it is a Fixed sign, the kind of feeling it projects may be described as introverted. Leo is Introverted Feeling.

Saying this troubles many people because they have an incorrect understanding of what is meant by the term introversion. They are so used to reading descriptions of this sign which portray its activity as highly extroverted for the reason that many Leo natives seem to lead rather notorious and public lives. But notoriety has nothing to do with introversion or extroversion. All that is meant by introversion is that of the motivation for actions, or behavior comes not from the outside world but is *subjectively conditioned*. In the case of Leo, it comes from some inner image, an idealized image of self which the person is always striving to become.

As for feeling, what is it that Leo does best? Projects feeling. This is the sign of the actor, the dramatist. An actor puts feeling into his words. Often there is an attraction to the theater or to film, and these people, whether they are performers or not—whatever their chosen field of action or profession—have a flair for drama, and for "making a production" of things. They put feeling into whatever they do.

There is a great need for recognition, appreciation, and applause, in Leo, to the extent that they may become disruptive in their efforts to command attention. Not always though, for often Leo can be very quiet and unobtrusive, nobly standing above the battle, refusing to be pulled into common conflict. An important thing we can learn from Leo is that whether or not we have done something heroic, magnificent, outstanding, or noteworthy, all, as mere human beings, deserve to be treated with honor and respect.

There is indeed a regal aspect to this sign, and, like all of the Fire signs, a considerable self-centeredness that can be very overbearing. A very proud sign is Leo, but as the saying goes, "Pride goeth before a fall," and because of this pride any comedown can be very painful indeed. Leo's feelings are easily hurt. Leo people can be very stubborn and inflexible.

The Lesser Benefic: The planet Venus is known as the Lesser Benefic. This too is her medieval title, and should be taken with a grain of salt. Venus is sister planet to Earth, and only slightly smaller. She is a glorious Morning or Evening Star and she is a beauty. Her nearness and her bright carbon-dioxide atmosphere cause her to appear larger and brighter than mighty Jupiter. Venus is the planet whose principle is pleasure, gratification, and money, but whether an emphasis on these matters is truly benefic is open to question. Corruption is a negative manifestation of this principle.

LIBRA: Libra is the seventh sign of the Zodiac. It is the sign that is introduced by the autumnal equinox. When the Sun enters 0 Libra, there is equal day and night once again, but now, the Sun is headed south of the Equator, and the days will gradually shorten and the nights grow longer until the longest night, the winter solstice. Libra is the first month of fall, and the first month of any season is characterized by much enthusiasm and excitement at the changes taking place in the Earth. As the Cardinal sign in the Air Triplicity Libra is the sign of Extroverted Thinking.

Meteorologists speak of this time as "the month of clear skies," and symbolically this may be taken to mean "clear thinking." Just as dense atmosphere clouds perception, clear atmosphere cleans it up. It is as if the cool, crisp breezes, of autumn abroad on the land were blowing away the summer dust and fuzzy cobwebs in our minds, allowing us to see more clearly.

That is the great gift of Libra. The ability to see, to understand, to clarify, to explain. Libra is a thinker-linker with the ability to show how one thing is related to another, and with a talent for mediation, an aptitude for understanding other people. It is a most charming and ingratiating trait. This is another of the "sweet" signs.

The danger in Libra is the tendency to be too reasonable, too understanding, too cooperative, and for this reason Libra can be taken advantage of. The wife who submits to abuse because she understands that the reason her husband abuses her is that he was an abused child is carrying the understanding of Libra to the extreme. The writer whose publisher says "Look, cash flow is tight, I can't give you a bigger advance," may not question the validity of that claim. Even Libra, which has a tendency to focus on the partner, has to say occasionally, "Hey, what about me?" But when that point has been reached, there is often a metaphorical hurricane that blows everything away and leaves devastation in its wake. For it is also true that Libra is literally the time of turbulent air and hurricanes, and tornadoes occur frequently when planets are in Libra.

There are two asteroids which may be said to rule Libra: Juno, the goddess of marriage and childbirth (she is also the goddess whom the winds obey), and Pallas, the goddess of wisdom and justice. Libra is the sign of relationship and the Zodiac symbol associated with this sign is Justice holding the scales. The Supreme Court does convene on the first Monday in October when the Sun is in Libra, and Librans are often attracted to the law.

Venus, who is usually named a ruler of this sign, has nothing to do with Libra. Venus is not the marrying kind, and whatever does this lazy goddess of pleasure have to do with justice?

Lights, the: The Sun and Moon are called the Lights, our day and night lights.

Longitude: Position on the Ecliptic measured from the first point of Aries or the vernal equinox.

Lord: The ruler of a sign. The "lord" of the horoscope is the planet that rules the Ascendant or Rising Sign. We don't use that term anymore.

Lucifer: "Light Bearer." A name for Venus when she is a morning star, rising before the Sun.

Lunation: The period of time during which the Moon progresses from one New Moon to another.

Major Aspects: 0 degrees—conjunction, 60 degrees—sextile, 90 degrees—square, 120 degrees—trine, and 180 degrees—opposition. (see Aspects)

Malefic: A medieval term, usually applied to certain conjunctions, oppositions, and squares. This is a term no longer acceptable because of its negative connotations. Nowadays we are more likely to call these aspects "difficult" or "inharmonious," but also strong, challenging, and potentially productive of achievement.

Mansions of the Moon: A system of signs found in Hindu and Chinese astrology, based on the Moon rather than the Sun.

MARS: The planet Mars is the fourth planet out from the Sun. It is the first planet whose orbit is extraterrestrial, that is, beyond that of Earth, and so, unlike Mercury and Venus, its position in the Zodiac is not limited by Earth's perspective. Mercury and Venus, which are intra-terrestrial planets, can never get very far from the Sun; Mars is able to be anywhere in the Zodiac relative to the Sun from the Earth's perspective.

Mars is much smaller than Earth and has a reddish color from the presence of iron on its surface. Kenneth F. Weaver reported (in National Geographic, August, 1970) the suggestion of Drs. William I. Plummer and Robert K. Carson that the reflection spectrum of Mars resembles that of an uncommon substance known as carbon suboxide, a foul-smelling compound. This led another scientist to suggest, "If you are planning to go to Mars, better take a clothespin for your nose. They tell me it smells like fermented sweatsocks."

Mars is inclined on its axis about 25 degrees to its orbital plane and so has seasonal variations like Earth. The eccentricity of its orbit gives the seasons varying lengths. Mars rotates on its axis in almost 25 hours. It has a very thin atmosphere, and because of this, Mars is unable to retain any of the Sun's energy. Though temperatures may go as high as 80 degrees at noon on its equator, that same spot will have lost about 100 degrees at midnight. Mars, unlike Venus, does not accumulate energy, it releases it. There may be water on Mars but it is eternally frozen—permafrost. It is a very desert-like body, with frequent violent windstorms that toss its surface material about, obliterating surface features. Mars has two satellites: Phobus and Deimos.

Mythologically, Mars is the god of war. He was the first-born of Jupiter and Juno. But it is also said that Mars had a twin sister Eris (Strife), and that they were conceived when Juno touched a certain flower. This warrior god had two attendants named Phobus and Deimos (Fear and Panic). It is also said that Mars loved battle for its own sake, delighting in the slaughter of men and the sacking of cities. All of his fellow immortals hated him, including his parents, except for three: Eris, his twin, Venus, who was intrigued by the powerful wild brute, and greedy Hades, who welcomed the bold young warriors slain by Mars in battle. He was not consistently victorious, however, and his macho manner often made him seem foolish and clumsy. Pallas Athena, the warrior maiden who sprang from the head of her father Jupiter, was a much more skillful fighter who occasionally bested Mars in battle. Once she kept him imprisoned in a bronze vessel for months. On another occasion Hercules sent him scurrying back to Mount Olympus in fear. He was the defendant in the very first trial for willful murder; that of Poseidon's son.

There are plenty of clues as to the nature of Mars in the above astronomical and mythological descriptions of this principle which are symbolic of, representatives of, or pointers to the matters over which the Planet has rulership.

We associate Mars and the sign Aries with the color red; the color of energy, of blood, the symbol for danger, and fire. The planet Mars is reddish in color. Mars is the ruler of the Aries Age, the Iron Age, and rusted iron is found on the surface of Mars. It is this rusted iron that gives Mars its reddish glow. The Aries Age, the Iron Age, came into being about 2500 BC. Metal artisans produced a new metal much harder than the bronze used since 3600 BC. Stronger weapons were made which empowered the period of empire building and conquest to come. Iron knives, swords, spears, arrows, and eventually guns and bullets, torpedoes, cannons, and bombs were to emerge. The materials and tools of war belong with Mars.

Mars is the principle of action, activity, and physical exertion, all of which require the spending, release, or consumption of energy. When we exercise, we generate heat and then we sweat in order to cool down. The planet Mars, because it has so slight an atmosphere, accumulates energy from the Sun, and at night, releases that energy and sends it unobstructed out into space. Mars heats up and cools down, like a desert where the days can be roasting hot and the nights very cold.

Active people generate and expend energy. All athletes do, as does anyone who must do heavy physical work. Psychologically, the emotions anger and fear generate heat, produce sweat, and stimulate adrenalin to cope with crises, followed by cooldown. Mars has to do with the "fight or flight" imperative. Fear and Panic are his attendants. Some of the words that describe Mars' activity include: short fused, rash, impulsive, impetuous, impatient, headstrong, chomping at the bit, sees red, shoots his bolt, blows off steam, steamed, fuming, fired up, on fire, burned up. Mars is the principle of action, initiative, self-assertion. It is a very valuable and essential principle. It is Mars that gets things started, that mobilizes us, that stimulates us to action, that helps us to fight to protect ourselves, to assert ourselves. He's a bit of a boor, but we need him.

Obviously, the mundane matters over which Mars and his sign Aries have rulership are: war, fire, extremes of heat and cold, and pioneering developments—first appearances of any kind. And in individual charts or lives, Mars is the principle of initiative and self-assertion.

MASCULINE: The masculine signs are the Fire signs: Aries, Leo, and Sagittarius, and the Air signs: Libra, Aquarius, and Gemini. These signs are Rational-Judgmental signs. With Fire

MASCULINE SIGNS

FIRE	AIR
♈ ♌ ♐	♊ ♎ ♒
FEELING	THINKING

RATIONAL-JUDGMENTAL

VALUATIONS	THOUGHTS
I	we
self	others
willful	reasonable
forceful	cooperative
self-centered	considerate
spirited	calming
self-involved	attentive
leader	counselor
impassioned	impersonal
contestant	mediator
self-assured	doubting
dramatize	clarify
being	meaning
performer	interpreter
desire	detachment
demonstrate	explain
prideful	unassuming
intense	casual
active	thoughtful
likes & dislikes	impartial
aspiring	communicating
sharing feelings	sharing thoughts
naive	knowing
self-sufficient	ingratiating
identity	relationship

signs judgments are made with regard to feelings, values, likes, and dislikes. And with Air signs, judgments are made with regard to thought, ideas, and rational understanding.

These signs are also called active-positive. Fire signs radiate and project, and Air signs cerebrate and reason.

Matutine: Planets and stars that are visible in the morning before sunrise are called matutine.

MEAN MOTION: The diurnal (daily) motion of the Sun, Moon, and planets. At different times in their orbits all of the heavenly bodies may move at differing speeds. Below is given the mean or average motion.

	Deg.	Min.	Sec.		
Sun	0	59	8 *		
Moon	13	10	35 *		
Mercury	0	84	0	Moves Retrograde for 24 days	Stationary for 1 Day Before and After Station
Venus	0	72	0	Moves Retrograde for 42 days	Stationary for 2 Days Before and After Station
Mars	0	31	0	Moves Retrograde for 80 days	Stationary for 2 – 3 Days Before and After Station
Asteroids	0	14	00	Moves Retrograde for 85 – 115 days	Stationary for 3 – 4 Days Before and After Station
Jupiter	0	4	59	Moves Retrograde for 20 days	Stationary for 5 Days Before and After Station
Saturn	0	2	1	Moves Retrograde for 140 days	Stationary for 5+ Days Before and After Station
Uranus	0	0	42	Moves Retrograde for 155 days	Stationary for 6 Days Before and After Station
Neptune	0	0	42	Moves Retrograde for 157 days	Stationary for 6+ Days Before and After Station

Pluto	0	0	48	Moves Retrograde for 160 days	Stationary for 8 Days Before and After Station

*The Sun and Moon are never Stationary or Retrograde.

These are all average diurnal motions and periods of Retrograde motion and duration of station. Because of the eccentricity of orbit there can be considerable variation in these numbers.

Medical Astrology: A specialized branch of astrology, for the practice of which there should also be considerable training and licensing in traditional medicine. If that is not the case, run the other way.

Medium Coeli: The M.C. or Midheaven. The highest point in the chart. The point directly overhead. The cusp of the Tenth House.

MERCURY: The solar system's innermost and smallest planet, Mercury is a rocky cinder cratered by comets and asteroids. It is a heavy and very dense planet, five and one half times as dense as water. Mercury is at one and the same time, the hottest and coldest of planets. On the day side temperatures reach 650 degrees Fahrenheit on the equator, and they probably drop to minus 300 degrees Fahrenheit on the nightside. There is apparently no atmosphere. Mercury reflects and polarizes light in a manner similar to that of the airless Moon. Mercury has a very eccentric orbit, and is inclined to the ecliptic by seven degrees.

In its relatively tiny orbit, this planet is so close to the Sun that most of the time it is swallowed up in the Sun's glare and is therefore seldom seen. On Earth, Mercury can sometimes be seen as a morning star (just before dawn) and as an evening star, but Earth's thick, hazy, and dust-filled atmosphere often blots it out. Elusive is Mercury.

It had always been believed that in its orbit Mercury kept the same face toward the Sun in its orbit. The widely held theory was that Mercury's rotation, like the Moon's was synchronous—that is, the body turned on its axis in just the same amount of time as it took to orbit the Sun. A period of 88 days. But in 1965 an amazing discovery was made. The huge radio telescope in Puerto Rico measured the planet's rotation (on its axis) at only 59 days, not 88. Astronomers were astonished. It is now realized that Mercury spins three times on his axis for every two revolutions about the Sun. So Mercury's year in 88 Earth days long, and its sidereal day (as seen from the stars) is 58.65 Earth days. But its solar day—that is, the period from one midnight or noon to the next—is exactly twice as long as its year, 176 Earth days. Tricky little rascal.

This strange combination of rotation and orbiting rates with an eccentric orbit brings about a very surprising effect in the apparent motion of the Sun over Mercury. If you were on Mercury at dawn just at perihelion passage, you would see the Sun come up, hang for a brief time in the sky [become Stationary], drop back below the horizon [turn Retrograde] then rise again [go Direct]. A sort of diurnal (Mercury's day) Retrograde motion of the Sun! This planet does have a very special relationship with the Sun.

Mythologically, Mercury (whose Greek name is Hermes) is the son of Jupiter and Maia. Immediately after his birth, he stole a herd of Apollo's cows (Apollo is the Sun-God) and constructed an ingenious musical toy from the shell of a tortoise and some cow gut—the lyre. Apollo was furious when he discovered who the thief was, and demanded that this herd be returned.

Mercury confessed and offered to return Apollo's herd. But when he took the lyre he had invented, he played such a ravishing tune on it, singing in praise of Apollo's nobility, intelligence and generosity, that of course he was forgiven at once. Apollo was so delighted he said, "You keep the cows, but give me the lyre." (That's a trade.)

Then, while the cows were grazing, Mercury cut reeds and made them into a shepherd's pipe and played another tune. Apollo was again delighted and cried, "If you give me that pipe, I will give you this golden staff with which I herd my cattle. In future you shall be the god of all herdsmen and shepherds." (So they made that trade, too.)

Apollo told Jupiter all about his rascally little son. The proud father was greatly amused and made Mercury his herald. Jupiter told him his duties would include the making of treaties, the promotion of commerce, and the maintenance of free rights of way for travelers on any road in the world. Jupiter gave him a herald's staff with white ribbons, which everyone was ordered to respect, a round hat against the rain, and winged golden sandals which carried him about with the swiftness of wind. Mercury promised he would "never tell lies, though I cannot promise always to tell the whole truth." Hades also engaged him as his herald, or as conductor of souls to the underworld.

The new little godling was welcomed into the Olympian family to whom he taught the art of making fire by the rapid twirling of the fire-stick. Afterwards the Thriae showed Mercury how to foretell the future from the dance of pebbles in a basin of water and he himself invented the game of knuckle-bones and the art of divining by them.

He then assisted the three Fates in the composition of the alphabet, invented astronomy, the musical scale, the arts of boxing and gymnastics, weights and measures, and the cultivation of the olive tree.

He had numerous sons among whom are: Echion, the Argonauts' herald; Autolycus, the thief; and Daphnis, the inventor of bucolic poetry. It is a mistake to think of this as a "neuter gender" kind of principle. This is a very phallic principle and, to some degree, also one of fertility. This is what "having numerous sons" means.

There are plenty of clues to the nature of Mercury in the above astronomical and mythological material concerning this principle. We must consider the astronomical facts and mythological stories as symbols, as representatives of or pointers to the matters over which the planet has rulership.

Astrologically, Mercury is a principle of perception. That Mercury has no atmosphere may very well be the astronomical indicator of clarity of perception. Atmosphere distorts perception. Think of the problems here on earth when astronomers try to see the stars and planets and galaxies through our atmosphere. Observatories are built on high mountains so as to get as far above the distorting atmosphere as possible in order to observe with greatest clarity.

Consider the fact that Mercury is the closest planet to the Sun and that mythologically, the Sun is represented by the god Apollo. It is interesting that astronomically Mercury has a special relationship to the Sun (on no other planet does the Sun rise twice) and mythologically his primary dealings are with Apollo, the Sun god. Since the Sun represents self, the perceptiveness of Mercury has to do with matters of greatest personal interest to self. Astrologically, the closer Mercury is to the Sun, the more subjective or self-centered is perception.

Mercury has the the fastest orbit—88 days. This rapid revolution of Mercury around the Sun means that Mercury will make all of the possible aspects to the other planets and asteroids faster and more frequently than any of the other bodies (except the Moon). An aspect between two bodies means information is shared, so we might say Mercury picks up and delivers information more quickly and more often than any of the other planets.

In the body, Mercury rules the nervous system, the system of pathways or network of nerves that carry messages and information to and from the brain, with the rapid transfer or transmission of information. The metal of Mercury is quicksilver. A very dense and very elusive metal. The planet Mercury is a very dense and very elusive body. It is a tragic fact that *mercury poisoning* has a most devastating effect on the nervous system.

More mundanely, Mercury is god of roads and highways, earth pathways along which may be conducted commerce, trade, the transport of goods of trade (the traveling salesman), and along which heralds, messengers, and scouts travel to carry and receive information. He does have to do with commerce for his business with Apollo was, after all, the first barter: "You may keep my cows, give me your lyre."

Mythologically, Mercury invented the alphabet. He was a great story teller. Very appropriately Mercury is the ruler of the Air sign Gemini, the sign of communication, information, news, letters, and language. Geminians often talk with their hands, as an accompaniment to their words. The deaf communicate with their hands of necessity; sign language also has an alphabet.

And Mercury has to do with the development of those skills that become automatic, that we take for granted, like talking, writing, walking, and using our hands on the typewriter as well as with other manual skills.

We know that Mercury has rulership over journalists, messengers, the telephone, and other more modern methods of communication, such as computers, fax machines, and satellites, which facilitate the most rapid methods of information transfer.

Mythologically, the speed of Mercury is symbolized by winged sandals (rapid transmission of information) and his perceptivity by the silver hat.

His staff with floating ribbons is really a magician's staff and is not the caduceus with coiled serpents which is associated with medicine. For on top of everything else, Mercury is a magician, skilled in prestidigitation. He has psychic gifts. Mercury invented the divining game of knuckle-bones and knew how to do augury from reading the patterns of pebbles dancing in a basin of water. The sign he rules, Gemini, is a double-bodied sign whose psychological functions are a blend of Thinking with Intuition. We often say of newsmen, "He has a nose for news," and since the nose is a symbol for intuition, what we are saying is, "That guy is pretty psychic." The Ouija board, Tarot cards, the pendulum, the divining rod, and automatic writing, are all divining devices whereby intuition is tapped, and these are under the aegis of Mercury and the sign he rules, Gemini.

Meridian: The great circle intersecting the Ecliptic which appears in a horoscope as a vertical line connecting the Midheaven and the Nadir. (see Circles)

Metals: The following are the metals most commonly linked to the planets:

Sun	— Gold
Moon	— Silver
Mercury	— Quicksilver
Venus	— Copper
Mars	— Iron
Jupiter	— Tin
Saturn	— Lead

With regard to the more recently discovered planets it seems logical to assign to

Uranus	— Uranium
Pluto	— Plutonium

But the metals associated with asteroids and Neptune have not been ascertained.

Midheaven: The Medium Coeli. The South angle or the cusp of the tenth house. The Zenith. (see Zenith)

Midpoint: A Midpoint is the ecliptic position midway between two points, such as two planets, a planet and ascendant, a planet and Midheaven. This is an aspect technique used primarily by the Uranian and Ebertin systems of astrology.

Milky Way: The Milky Way is our home galaxy, in which our Sun is an average star on the fringe of its spiral. Mythologically, the Milky Way is said to have been formed when the infant Hercules was placed at Juno's breast as she slept, but when she awoke she pushed the child away and the milk thus spilled and spread through the heavens and created the Milky Way. However, his having nursed at the breast of the goddess, if only for a moment, is said to account for Hercules' prodigious strength.

Moisture: Moisture is said to abound when planets are matutine, when the Moon is in her first quarter, and during the winter and the night.

MOON: Our one and only most amazing non-man-made Earth satellite, the Moon magically is just the right size and distance from the Earth so that when it is on the ecliptic and new, the incredible phenomenon of the total solar eclipse occurs. Then our small Moon perfectly covers our giant Sun, so that both bodies appear to be the identical size. If the eclipse is total, the Sun will reveal his magnificent corona and on earth we may actually see the shadow of the Moon cast by the Sun racing eastward at the rate of between 18 to 40 miles a minute depending on how close to the equator the shadow falls. The Moon is the fastest-moving celestial body up there.

The Moon is one quarter of the Earth's diameter, 3476 km. Actually rather large for a satellite, it is about 30 Earth diameters away from us.

The Moon exerts tidal forces on the Earth. These result in ocean tides associated with the Moon, with typically two high tides and two low tides occurring each day.

The Moon has much in common with Mercury. Like Mercury, she has no atmosphere to speak of, which means no insulation to protect against the intense heat of the Sun, or to keep the heat accumulated from the Sun from drifting out into space at night. Thus extremes of temperature are common to both bodies. The temperature on the Moon ranges from just above the boiling point of water where the Sun shines to about 173 Centigrade on the dark side.

No atmosphere and no wind and water erosion, permit the Moon and Mercury to retain evidence of their physical history. The astronauts footprints on the Moon will be there forever.

The Moon is cratered and pitted like Mercury, but unlike Mercury rotates only once on her axis in her 29.5 Earth day orbit of the Earth, and therefore keeps only one face toward Earth. Her other side is never visible to us, though it is to the sun.

The Moon does not radiate her own light. She is a mirror, a reflector of sunlight. Unlike Mercury, who is so elusive, the moon is a very visible body; she is our night light and at times reflects enough sunlight for us to read by.

The lunar goddess is Artemis (Diana). She is closely associated with Selene and Hecate. These are probably the three aspects of the Moon goddess, three personalities of the one archetype. Selene in Heaven (the actual globe of the Moon as Helios is the actual globe of the Sun), Artemis on Earth (the fleet-footed huntress), and Hecate in the infernal regions. Hecate may represent the dark (to us) side of the Moon or the

Moon in her invisible phases (associated with Hades and Persephone).

Apollo and Artemis are the twin children of Leto (the consequence of her rape by Jupiter). Artemis was born first and without travail, and immediately helped her mother with the delivery of her twin, Apollo. Thus Artemis is known as a goddess of childbirth. She shared similar attributes with Apollo; both were armed with bow, quiver, and arrows, and both sent plagues and death among men and animals.

Apollo and Artemis are light deities. He rules the day, she the night. She has to do with nocturnal phenomena, with the enchantment of the moonlight, and with dew which is most profuse on clear moonlit nights. She is goddess of waters and tides and is protectress of fishermen, guardian of harbors. She is protectress of little children and of all sucking animals, but she also loves the chase, especially that of stags. She is goddess of the hunt and protectress of herds from beasts of prey. Women in labor often invoked her, since her mother Leto carried and bore her without pain and the Fates made her patroness of childbirth. Jupiter decreed that she too, like Mercury, would be guardian of roads and harbors.

The Cyclopes, who are smithies made her a silver bow with a quiverful of arrows (her silver bow stood for the New Moon, the arrows for her shafts of moonlight). The god Pan, who raised hunting dogs, gave her a baker's dozen of fine, swift hunters.

She was a scrupulously chaste goddess and required the same perfect chastity from her companions as she did of herself.

Artemis is described by Homer as a lioness (they do hunt at night). The classical Artemis was a goddess of wildlife and especially the young of all living things.

Artemis' connection with the life of women led to her identification with the Moon. The Moon was thought to exercise a powerful influence over the physical life of women, the lunar cycle of 29 days corresponding to a woman's menstrual cycle.

The cult of this goddess was exported to such places as Ephesus, a city in Asia-Minor, where she was worshipped in a great temple that became known as one of the seven wonders of the world. At Ephesus there is a famous statue of Diana, a many-breasted mother figure whose robe contains the images of many wild animals.

There are many clues to the nature of the Moon in the above astronomical and mythological material concerning this principle. We must consider the astronomical facts and mythological stories as symbols, as representatives of or pointers to the matters over which the celestial body has rulership.

Let us consider the importance of the absence of atmosphere and the nature of perception. The Moon shares this absence of atmosphere with Mercury, but while Mercury seems to represent self-conscious perception because of his proximity to the Sun, the Moon seems to have more to do with our instinctive perception and conditioning. Is this because she is Earth-bound while Mercury is Sun-bound? She also has a very close association with wild animals, the course of whose lives is totally conditioned by their instinctive intelligence.

Both Mercury and the Moon are heavily cratered. Astrologers are aware that memory is associated with the Moon, and probably with Mercury, too. It could be that this attribute is confirmed very dramatically by the picture of the astronaut's footprint on the Moon. That footprint, like the crater markings from ages and ages ago, will stay there forever unless obliterated by another bombardment of debris from space. There is no atmosphere, no wind, no water to erode the marks left by impacts on the Moon. The Moon remembers.

The powerful effect of the Moon on the waters of the Earth is very significant. The Moon moves water, sets it in motion, tugs and pulls at it, creates our tides. Water responds to the pull of the Moon. Water is symbolic of emotion. Therefore the Moon is the indicator of our emotional response to things. In the myth, the wild animals also symbolize emotions—wild uncontrollable, instinctive emotions. It is an accepted fact that at the time of the Full Moon (full emotion), police stations and hospital emergency rooms have a rush of activity precipitated by persons unable to control the emotions which have overwhelmed them.

Flood tides also are symbolic of being overwhelmed by or flooded with emotion. The Moon rules the sign Cancer, a highly emotional, responsive, reactive sign, which is initiated at the summer solstice; summertime, when water is especially dear to us.

The Moon is the fastest-moving body up there. Diana the huntress races with her hounds. Because she is the fastest body, the moon makes more aspects more frequently to all of the other planets. This rapid shifting from one aspect to another represents the rapid shifting of moods and emotions that the moon represents. The Moon is moody.

The sunlight reflected by the Moon has the same spectrum analysis as the Sun itself. Diana and Apollo are twins, with much in common, only she rules the night and he the day. They both have bows and arrows, and these symbolize or represent the rays of sunlight and moonlight.

As Diana is goddess of the young of all living things and of sucking creatures, we should see the Moon as a nurturing principle, but with regard to the very young to newborn humans, infantile and dependent and therefore still functioning on a totally instinctive level, like the little animals. She provides liquid nourishment.

The dark side of the Moon: That which is hidden is always suggestive of mystery, magic, the occult. This is the Hecate aspect of the Moon, the association with Hades and Persephone, with the underworld, and with witchcraft.

Motion: Planets move at varying speeds in their orbits. But each has a mean motion. If they exceed their mean motion they are said to be moving quickly. If they fall short, they are said to be moving slowly. (see Mean Motion)

Mundane Astrology: Mundane means "in the world." This is a kind of astrology that deals with happenings, events, and developments in various countries, cities, and states rather than with personalities and individuals, unless those individuals have impact on world events in some tangible way, as, for example, prime ministers or presidents of countries.

MUTABLE SIGNS: These are the third signs of each season: Gemini, Virgo, Sagittarius, and Pisces. This is the Mutable or Common Quadrature—one Air, one Earth, one Fire, and one Water—four different elements, but of the same general attitude type.

In the third month of each season the Earth can't seem

to make up its mind whether to stay in the season it is in or to move into the coming season. That is why we say that March, when the Sun is in Pisces, "comes in like a lion and goes out like a lamb" and why, in June, when the Sun is in Gemini in the midst of a series of balmy spring-like days, it is suddenly summer. It is why we find certain days in September, when the Sun is in Virgo, to be hot as the hottest days in summer, and others when we could swear that fall has surely arrived; and why, in December, when the Sun is in Sagittarius, a sudden snowstorm will engulf us in the deep freeze of winter.

We call these signs "dual" or "double-bodied," because more than one thing is going on in them—more than one season and more than one psychological function. Gemini, which is an Air sign and therefore thinking, is headed toward the Cardinal Water sign Cancer, a very intuitive sign; so Gemini is a blending of thinking and intuition—Thinking-Intuition. Virgo is an Earth sign and therefore represents the function sensation, but it is headed toward the thinking Air sign Libra, so Virgo is a combination of Sensation-Thinking, or thinking in relation to things.

Sagittarius is a Fire sign and represents the psychological function feeling, but it is headed toward the very physical Earth sign Capricorn, so Sagittarius is a blending of the psychological functions, Feeling-Sensation. Pisces, a Water sign, is primarily intuition, but its approach to Aries links the two functions—intuition with feeling—Intuitive-Feeling.

After Jung's disciple, Erich Neumann, I have been calling the general attitude manifested by this Quadrature of signs " Centroverted" because an Extroverted (Cardinal) sign is on

126

one side and an Introverted (Fixed) sign is on the other. These Mutable signs have in common the great need for people with whom to share their interests. They share their perceptions in Gemini, their work in Virgo, their feelings and enthusiasms in Sagittarius, and their empathy and emotions in Pisces. They are "me too" signs; they tend to be very personal and much interested in personality. They are neither introverted nor extroverted but their actions are determined by both inner and outer, subjective and objective considerations.

Mutual Reception: When two planets are in each other's signs, they are said to be in mutual reception, i.e., Mars in Capricorn is in Saturn's sign; Saturn in Aries is in Mars' sign; Mercury in Sagittarius is in Jupiter's sign; Jupiter in Gemini is in Mercury's sign.

This condition establishes a relationship between the two planets even if they are not in aspect. It intensifies the connection if they are. (see Sign Rulerships)

MYTHOLOGY: The planets we use in astrology represent different principles of energy. Each planet is an archetype of a specific kind of activity—an activity so unique, so specialized, that no other planet can be the carrier of these specific qualities. Further, each planet comprises a variety of characteristics; gifts, virtues, and faults so appropriate to that particular principle as to constellate a personality, a particular god, or an archetype. The mythological gods whose names were given to the planets are the very same principles which the planets represent. It is possible that the gods emerged as archetypes of the qualities which the planets described . . . ! First came the observation of the planet and its influence over the

centuries, then gradually, the personality that most completely embodied the qualities of each planet appeared as a god in
religious and mythological phenomena.

But how to explain the fact that although all mythologies
have hundreds of gods, hundreds of archetypes, we astrologers
used only seven gods in our art—the seven celestial bodies—
the Sun and Moon (Apollo and Diana) and the five planets,
Mercury, Venus, Mars, Jupiter, and Saturn—until 1781, when
Uranus was discovered? I believe that the other planets (gods),
all of them, to the tiniest pebble in the Asteroid Belt, *were* "observed," were "seen"! For when I speak of observation and seeing in ancient times I do not believe that this seeing had to
be with the eye, naked or otherwise. "See'ers" (seers) are psychics, and those who were around in that long ago time were
aware of the celestial principles. They could "see" (intuit) the
planets (the gods) long before their discovery was made possible through the technological developments which now enable
us to see galaxies billions of light years away. These seers, ora-
cles, spiritual leaders, priest[esses], shamans, and prophets, developed the pantheon of the gods of which we read in the
myths and religions of all peoples. The astronomers who "discovered" hitherto unknown planets, and named them, were
in the special position of bringing into consciousness principles which were known eons ago. However, the world was not
really ready to deal with them until the actual discovery of the
newer planets (the bearers of the archetypes) brought these principles into overt consciousness. The astronomers discovered and
identified, or named, the archetypes that the newly-discovered
planets represented, never knowing they were instruments chos-

en to aid in the expansion of consciousness which any newly-discovered planet will effect.

Of course there are no gods. These wonderful mythological personalities are constructs: perfect personifications of abstract principles, those basic principles upon which all life depends. It's foolish to think of them as actual beings, but it is impossible to resist the temptation to do so.

The planets are named after the gods and goddesses of ancient Greece and Rome. We astrologers do not believe that that ruddy ball rolling around up in the heavens really is a god, or even that it is merely the domain of a god—the god Mars, that energetic warrior of ancient Rome. But we do know that the principle this planet represents astrologically is the same as that of the god, Mars. The planet and the god represent the same archetype—action, aggression, energy, self-assertion, initiative, impatience. We know this to be so from observation. We have also observed that the planet Venus represents Venusian matters—love, gratification, pleasure, desire; that Jupiter represents Jovian matters, enthusiasm, bombast, expansion; that Saturn represents contraction, crystallization, sensitivity, etc. So it is with all of the planets: They all represent one or another specific principle of energy that accords with the mythological archetype for which they are named, and for which no other celestial body can speak.

This connection of planet with mythological archetype became especially helpful with the discovery of the new planets Uranus, Neptune and Pluto, and especially with the discovery of the asteroids. The asteroids were given the names of four great goddesses by the astronomers who discovered them.

Whatever their reasons for assigning the names they did to these new planets, the astronomers were unwittingly identifying an archetype. For these four new bodies do represent four aspects of the feminine principle, aspects that the Moon and Venus do not encompass. The mythology surrounding these goddesses opened the door to understanding the significance of these new bodies—Ceres, Pallas, Juno and Vesta. Based on the myths, we developed hypotheses as to their function and after much study and observation, we were able to confirm the validity of our speculations.

Thus the myths enlighten us through symbol and metaphor as to the principles that the gods and the planets represent. They are enormously helpful to astrologers striving to penetrate the mystery we are confronted with when new planets are discovered or when new discoveries are made about the planets (principles) with which we are already familiar.

NADIR: The bottom—the lowest point in the heavens, opposite the Midheaven or Zenith. Actually, in a horoscope, it is the lowest point in the celestial sphere under the earth. That celestial sphere is all around us: we, the Earth, are just a teeny-weenie little spot in the center of it all.

Native: The person for whom the horoscope was set.

Nativity: The birth. A horoscope set for the time of birth. The birth chart of the native.

Nebulae: Fuzzy clusters of stars that have the appearance of clouds. The belief about the astrological significance of these star clusters is another example of medieval madness. The claim was made that if one of these nebulae was rising or with the Moon at birth this would cause blindness or some other ocular defect. Very imaginative, those old-timers. We know now that those clusters of stars are giant galaxies of billions of stars: they are unimaginable distances away from us and there are vast numbers of them. But they have nothing to do with blindness. If they did, we'd all be blind.

NEPTUNE: Neptune, like Uranus and the asteroids, is a relative newcomer to astrology. He was discovered September 23, 1846, from the observatory in Berlin. Two astronomers share credit for his discovery: Leverrier and Adams.

Neptune is almost 30 times as far from the Sun as we are. It takes Neptune 165 years to complete one revolution around the Sun and this, the first revolution since his discovery, will not be complete until 2011. This means that whenever Neptune moves into a new sign, we, never having experienced him in that sign before, will learn new things about that planet and the nature of his manifestation in this new sign. The pioneering journey of Neptune is still in progress, and we are now learning about how he will manifest in the sign Capricorn.

Neptune's day is 15.8 hours. Pretty fast rotation, considering this is such a large body. His mass is 17.2 times that of Earth, and he does have seasons in the usual sense, that is, having changing meteorological conditions, for his axis is inclined to his orbit about 29 degrees. Neptune appears telescopically as a small, fuzzy, greenish disc, the light of which is reflected from a gaseous atmosphere. Like the other Jovians, he has a ring system and a family of satellites.

He has an almost perfectly circular orbit, a condition he shares with Venus. This is interesting in that Neptune is said to be the "higher vibration" of Venus, whatever that means.

Neptune is a twin planet to Uranus and has much in common with that planet but is also so very different, as you will see when you read about Uranus. Two important differences from Uranus are: Neptune has internal heat and gives off 2.8 times as much energy as it receives from the Sun. Uranus doesn't. And the gas ethane has been detected on Neptune; not on Uranus.

At present Neptune is the most distant planet in the solar system. But that is not Neptune's doing, for his orbit is not eccentric. It is instead due to the eccentric orbit of Pluto, which is really the furthermost planet in the solar system, but which edged inside the orbit of Neptune in 1979 and will remain inside until March 1999.

Mythologically, after Jupiter, Pluto, and Neptune (their Roman names) deposed their father Saturn, they, like thieves dividing the spoils, shook lots in a helmet to see who would be Lord of the sky, the underworld, and the sea. Neptune got the sea. He had no right to it, for the sea is a feminine element and Amphitrite was already the goddess of the sea. But those three brothers were taking over (patriarchy was rearing its ugly head). Neptune thought it would be a good arrangement if he took Amphitrite for his consort, but she found him so repugnant she ran away when he approached her. Later, seduced by the sweet words of Delphinus, who, like Cyrano for Christian, pled for Neptune so persuasively, she consented. They had three sons. Neptune, like Jupiter, was a bit of a philanderer and caused Amphitrite much grief.

Robert Graves tells us that this character was greedy of earthly kingdoms and claimed possession of Attica by thrusting his trident into the Acropolis at Athens where a well of sea-water immediately gushed out and is still to be seen. Athena also claimed possession of Attica and planted the first olive tree beside the well. Neptune was furious and would have fought her, but Jupiter interposed and ordered that they submit the dispute to arbitration. The upshot was that Athena was deemed to have the better right to the land because she had given the better gift. Neptune was a sore loser and sent huge waves to flood the Thracian plain. There are at least five other occasions when he tried to seize other lands but was unsuccessful. He was forbidden to use flood as revenge as he did before so he did the exact opposite; he dried up the streams so that they never flow now in summer. On the other hand, for the sake of one of the Danaids who were distressed by the dried-up streams, he caused the Argive river of Lerna to flow perpetually. (Apparently streams and rivers are also in the sphere of Neptune.)

He boasted of having created the horse, but that isn't so, though his claim to have instituted horse-racing is not disputed. He also claimed to have invented the bridle, but Athena did that before him.

Astrologically, Neptune does have to do with matters that relate to water, especially the rivers, streams, and currents of water on land and in the oceans. But Neptune also has to do with air currents and rivers of air in the ether as well. Mark Edmund Jones has told us that Neptune has to do with airplane travel.

The Neptune idea may be understood by imagining a toy boat being set adrift on a little stream and being carried along to where it joins a larger stream or river which finally leads to entry into the ocean. Being carried by, going along with, rhythmical flow, yielding to the flow of the current. That is Neptune. On the water or in the air, one has given up control and is being carried by other forces than self.

Neptune is the planet of conformity and often of dependence, and that is where he is so different from Uranus, the planet of individuality and independence. Neptune is herd instinct: a herd of sheep, a school of fish, a flock of geese. This is not necessarily negative. Experiences as sublimely wonderful as a sense of union with God, total egolessness, wholeness, being a part of everything, everything a part of self, or as destructive as the mass suicide of the deluded followers of Jim Jones, escape into alcoholic or drugged lethargy, indifference, irresponsibility, confusion, and delusion, may be had with Neptune aspects. It really means giving up control, letting go, being carried by . . . and so on. Being able to believe something is so when it isn't. This is imagination, fantasy. So Neptune rules all things that induce illusion, fantasy, and emotional responses to things that are not really there. When you watch a movie, you are looking at images on a wall that is in reality blank, but you may be laughing or crying, for you will have given yourself over to the illusion, you will have lost yourself. When you look at a photo, it is not the real person or place, but it can awaken the presence of that person it represents as though they are really there.

Neptune rules music (which we must allow to carry us if we really want to hear it). Neptune has to be prominent in the charts of musicians, photographers, filmmakers, and advertising people (ads are illusion). Neptune, of course, as ruler of Pisces, rules the feet, and so we often find dancers with Neptune or Pisces emphasized in their charts.

Neptune rules chemicals generally and, most notoriously, alcohol and drugs, which may induce illusion or merely enable us to shed our inhibitions and controls. But there may be important and very valuable and magical developments in the field of chemistry with Neptune stations and aspects.

Neptune has to do with matters that concern water and water agencies; too much or too little water, flooding, drought, water in the atmosphere that clouds perception, mistiness, fogginess, and all situations where one does not see straight, either because of mist or fog or a befogged perceptive function such as rose-tinted glasses, willfully looking the other way, not seeing what is really there, or clouded perception due to drugs.

Of course, maritime matters are in the sphere of Neptune.

Marc Jones speaks of Neptune as the planet of obligation or escape from obligation. Thus, at times we may witness heroic self-giving, self-sacrifice to the point of martyrdom with aspects involving Neptune or, on the other hand, utter irresponsibility and escape from obligation.

NEW MOON: The moment when the Moon is in conjunction with the Sun (strictly, having the same ecliptic longitude), passing north or south of, and sometimes eclipsing it.

Newton: Sir Isaac Newton (1642 – 1727). The British scientist who discovered the Laws of Motion and Gravity. He shattered the age-old separation of the Earth and the heavens by linking the Earth's gravity (terrestrial physics) to the orbital motion of the planets (celestial physics).

Ninety Degree Dials: (see Uranian System)

Nocturnal Arc: The time it takes a planet to progress from its setting to its rising. This may be expressed in time or in equivalent degrees and minutes of a circle. In either case, it is right ascension and is measured on the Equator.

NODES: Lunar Nodes: the points where the Moon in her orbit cuts across the path of Earth's orbit, the Ecliptic. When she is heading north of the Ecliptic, that point is called North Node, Caput Draconis, or Dragon's Head, and, when she is heading south, that point is called South Mode, Cauda Draconis, or the Dragon's Tail.

Planetary Nodes: These are the points at which the planets in their several orbits cross the Ecliptic, for of course the planets, too, have a north and a south node. The planes of their orbits are inclined to the Ecliptic at varying angles. The nodes of each planet are not fixed; they undergo a gradual change over time.

The North and South Nodes are like the vernal and autumnal equinoctial points (zero degrees of Aries and zero degrees of Libra) in the Sun's journey through the signs, but relative to the Moon and planets.

Many astrologers find the Moon's nodes extremely important in delineation. But their explanations of this significance vary. Generally, it is thought that the North Node is a point of instinctive self-protection, and the South Node is a place of letting things "go to pot." Whether this is thought to be the case with the planets' North and South Nodes, I do not know. Most astrologers have not studied this aspect of planetary interpretation. Perhaps more will be done, for the most recent computer programs do include the North and South Nodes of the planets.

North Pole: The star Polaris marks the North Pole of the celestial sphere. It is the extension of the Earth axis to that point in the heavens which appears to be stationary, around which everything else revolves. Due to precession of the equinoxes, this North Pole point shifts over time, and eventually some other star will be our North Pole marker.

Northern Signs: These are the signs from Aries to Virgo. They used to be called commanding signs. Their opposites, Libra to Pisces, are southern signs, formerly called obeying signs. I don't think anybody knows why they were thus called. It doesn't make sense to me.

Occidental—Oriental: Occidental means westerly. Literally "falling down." The west is where planets set. It is the opposite of oriental, which means easterly, where planets rise. With regard to the Sun, planets that rise after the Sun are said to be oriental, and planets that have risen before the Sun are called occidental. Medieval astrology probably attributed some special arcane significance to these oriental or occidental positions.

Occultation: Astronomically, when the Moon passes over the Sun, it is called an eclipse. But when she passes over a planet, an asteroid, a comet, or a star, that is called an occultation. Planets, too, may occult other planets or stars. I suppose occult means hidden, to hide, which is what happens. Astronomers learn a lot about stars and planets through these occultations. Astrologers could learn something about the principles that the stars or planets represent at these occultations if they were aware of them, which they usually are not.

Opposition: (see Aspects)

Orbit: Path in space taken by a body (such as a planet, or comet, or an artificial satellite) moving around another body (such as the Sun or the Earth). Its shape is one of the conic sections; an ellipse if the orbit is closed; a hyperbola if it is temporary and open.

Orbs of Planets: (see Aspects)

Orion: The constellation. The heavenly hunter with his snazzy belt. This constellation is found in the vicinity of Gemini. Two bright stars Rigel and Bellatrix are found in this constellation, as is Betelgeuse too.

PALLAS: Pallas was the third asteroid to be discovered. She is next in size to Ceres, about 304 miles in diameter. Pallas has a very eccentric orbit which brings her closer to Jupiter than any of the other three asteroids. She has a special relationship to Jupiter in that her period is in an 18 to seven ratio with his. That is, for every seven orbits of Jupiter, Pallas will have made 18. Since her orbit takes 4.61 Earth years to complete, that equals 83 years. So every 83 years both Pallas and Jupiter will have stations in almost exactly the same degrees and signs. She is the only one with such a relationship to Jupiter and this is interesting in that mythologically she is his beloved daughter. She is inclined to the ecliptic more than any other planet—almost 35 degrees—and rotates on her axis in five and one-half hours.

Pallas is the goddess of wisdom and justice and shares the rulership of Libra with Juno. The myth says that Pallas was born from the head of Jupiter, a symbolic way of saying that she is "of the mind." (It is also a theological device to arrogate wisdom as emanating from the masculine.) She is the "brainchild" of Jupiter. She is said to have invented the spinning wheel, the potters wheel, architecture, and ship design. She was a weaver of tapestries, she harnessed the horse, domesticated animals, created the olive tree. She was an excellent strategist, and much more.

Pallas is a principle of intelligence, ingenuity, excellence. She represents the ability to think, to link, to make connections (to weave), to see how one thing is related to another, to make judgments, to reason and understand. She has to do with pattern perception and pattern creation.

Unlike Mercury, she is more than mere perception. Her expertise is not limited to communication, information, manual dexterity. Nor is she the nervous system, relaying messages and information to and from the brain: she is the brain itself. And unlike Mercury, there are moral connotations to her thinking. Mercury is amoral, he is a liar and a thief. He does not make judgments. Mercury simply perceives, reports, records. He doesn't care one way or the other about the issues. Pallas *understands* what she is perceiving. That is what the symbolism of weaving represents. She gets the picture, makes connections, and she makes a judgment.

This principle of intelligence enables us to use our brains, to solve problems, to find better ways of doing things. It is Pallas who is the inventor, not Uranus, as we have always been told, because inventions are always in the interest of solving problems and greater efficiency, and Pallas is an efficiency principle. Uranus does have to do with electricity, electronics, and science, but it it Pallas who found ways of putting electricity to use, and who used science to advance invention and efficiency. It is Pallas who incorporated Uranus into the economy. Uranus turns lights on, awakens us. He is revolutionary, but is not in the least interested in economics or efficiency unless he is linked to Pallas. If you are talking revolution, that's Uranus, but when you specify "industrial" you've brought Pallas into the picture.

Pallas is a principle of technology. Thus when it is said that she created or invented the olive, this should be taken to mean she introduced a *technology* which enhanced the production of olives. That is, olive trees that develop from seed alone produce very poor or scanty fruit. The trees which are grafted, however, are lush and are incredibly more productive of fruit. This grafting technique was imported from Libya in ancient times, and Libya is the place where the concept of Pallas Athene originated.

As an economics principle, Pallas is of necessity an urban deity, for cities are economic centers. Pallas is goddess of cities. She is a city slicker. She has "street smarts."

Pallas, like the other goddesses, existed long before the arrival of the Aries Age and patriarchy. Since the mythological references to her come from the Aries Age, it is easy to be misled into thinking of her only as a "warrior maiden." No doubt her intelligence and wise strategy were put to work by the Aries Age generals and warriors, but in other ages her intelligence found expression in other areas than war and conquest.

Pallas carries a shield and wears a goatskin tunic fringed with serpents and with the hideous face of Medusa on it. The meaning in this symbolism is very interesting. It means "repellent power," shielding, self protection, defense. She would be more involved with defensive strategy than with aggressive war. But on the microscopic level, I believe this shielding function has to do with the immune system which protects the body against "invasion." Pallas would be the indicator of vaccines, anti-toxins, substances that can protect the body.

PARALLELS: There are two kinds of parallels: zodiacal, as when two bodies have the same number of degrees of declination, either north or south of the Equator, or mundane, when two bodies are at the same distance from opposite sides of one of the four angles of the horoscope. These parallels are thought to be as effective as conjunctions by some astrologers.

Parents: Usually the tenth house denotes the mother, and the fourth house the father. The tenth house is the place of authority in the chart and the mother is the initial authority in relation to the child. It usually falls to the mother to be that parent who says, "No," to be "she who must be obeyed." In adulthood the tenth house represents all those whom the native considers to be authority figures, especially the employer.

The fourth house usually designates the father, the one who generally provides for the child's basic security.

In our time the assignment of mother to the tenth house and father to the fourth house is running less and less according to expectation. There is an increasing parent reversal effect as both mothers and fathers take up the duties of both parents when there is a divorce. Whoever has custody of the children must fulfill the roles of both parents.

In trying to identify the parents in the horoscope, we look for the rulers of the signs on the cusps of the tenth and fourth houses of the birth chart. Any planets contained in those houses contribute further descriptive elements concerning the parents.

This astrologer does not accept the common proposition that the Moon represents the mother and Saturn the father, simply because the Moon rules Cancer, the fourth sign of the Zodiac, and Saturn rules Capricorn, the tenth sign. In the first place, both Cancer and Capricorn are feminine signs, and Saturn is merely the patriarchal, Aries Age stand-in for the Great Goddess of the Mountain. The astrological implication here is that the original family group consisted of mother and child, with the mother performing both parental functions. It may be that father-parenting is a fairly recent phenomenon in human history. There was a time when men were not aware of their part in conception, and the miracle of birth was thought to be the province of women alone.

Pars Fortuna, Part of Fortune: (see Arabic Parts)

Partile Aspect: Two planets that are exactly in the same degree and minute of the same sign; a very exact conjunction.

Penumbral Eclipse: This is simply an eclipse that is partial (Latin-paene, "almost"). The Moon will cover the Sun, but a portion of the Sun will still be visible. The total eclipse is much more dramatic.

Perigee: This is when the Moon and planets come closest to earth in their orbits.

Perihelion: When the Earth and planets are closest to the Sun in their orbits.

Periodical Lunation (Lunar Return): The monthly return of the Moon to the very sign, degree and minute that it was in at birth. Some astrologers use this for monthly forecasts in the same manner as they do solar returns for the time each year when the Sun returns to where it was at birth.

Persona: One's public image, the mask one wears, so to speak. Various astrologers have differing opinions about where to locate this aspect of identity in the horoscope. Many say it is found at the Ascendant. I believe it is more appropriate to locate it at the Midheaven, the 10th house. For aside from indicating one of the parents (usually the mother) and the employer, the 10th house also indicates the figure one cuts in the world, one's public image, in short, the persona. When this is emphasized in the chart, one is very closely identified with one's profession: one is one's profession.

PISCES: Pisces is the last sign of the Zodiac, the third sign of the winter season, and therefore a double-bodied, or Mutable sign. And just as the season is losing its wintry power—the snow is beginning to melt, ice is breaking up in lakes and ponds, floes are flowing, blustery winds with a hint of spring are blowing—so within the human psyche is there an adjustment being made between the season of winter and the coming season of spring. March comes in like a lion and goes out like a lamb (Aries).

This is a Water sign, and the three Water signs are aspects of the psychological function intuition. But since this is a Mutable sign, it is also borrowing some of its function from the Fire sign to which it is applying, Aries. And so Pisces is a blend of intuition with feeling—it describes the psychological function Intuitive-Feeling.

This is the sign of empathy and compassion, the native often so attuned to others that s/he feels their pain or sorrow or joy as though it is happening to the self. This is a self-losing, self-giving, merging, blending with whatever is going on in the vicinity kind of sign. Often this tendency is perceived as a problem of identity because of the inclination to live life through others. But perhaps this highly intuitive gift of empathy should be seen as an *aspect* of the native's identity, and not as a flaw, provided it is not carried to the extreme.

Pisces is imaginative, emotional, responsive to rhythmical flow, and therefore to music, dance, and the rippling waves of water. Water is a magical lure to Pisceans and they are often found in the Navy, interested in water sports, or inclined to leisurely showers. They are water-babies. These people are also attracted to film and photography, for through these media illusion appears to be real. Pisces people have great imaginations and are very responsive to illusion. Yielding to illusion is another way of losing the self, or of self-giving.

There are constructive ways of losing the self; in one's work, where the work itself is more important than the ego of the worker; in spiritual experience, where there is a sublime sense of oneness with God—mystical egolessness, called Nirvana in the east; in allowing oneself to be a medium, a receiver of knowledge, information, or artistry from the great collective unconscious—like an Einstein, an Edgar Cayce, or a Michelangelo.

There are some very destructive ways of losing self: alcohol, drugs, and other chemicals; though Pisceans have no need to enhance their imagination through synthetic means, still they can be seduced into using them. Curiously, there can be a great scientific interest in chemistry in this sign.

Self-giving and self-losing can also be self-sacrifice. The sign

Pisces has defined this current age which is fast approaching it's end; the almost 2,000 year period that was initiated with the sacrifice on the cross, the Christian era. There is sometimes an unwholesome penchant for martyrdom or self-pity in this sign to which its members need to be alerted.

Obviously, Neptune is the ruler of the sign Pisces.

Planetary Hours: Certain hours of the day are governed by certain planets or Lights. The first hour after sunrise is governed by the planet that gives its name to that day: Sun for Sunday, Moon for Monday, Mars for Tuesday, Mercury for Wednesday, Jupiter for Thursday, Venus for Friday, and Saturn for Saturday. The rest of the planets follow in order, according to the Chaldean arrangement, which has respect to the apparent velocities of the planets, namely, Saturn, Jupiter, Mars, Sun, Venus, Mercury, Moon, and so round again in the same order.

Hence as there are 24 hours and seven planets, the latter will be contained three times and three over, and this brings us to the 25th hour which is the first hour of the next day and is found to be ruled by the planet whose name it bears.

A planet that is in good aspect to the Moon on any day will bring good fortune to those who act during its hours on that day, especially if it is also the ruler of the day. But when the ruling planet of the hour is in bad aspect to the Moon it is better to let others act and so avoid the greater measure of ill.

All this was figured out by some imaginative astrologers before the discovery of Uranus, the asteroids, Neptune, and Pluto. You will have noticed that they are not included in these planetary hours. So, what do you think? Are you going to take it seriously? Are you going to run your life according to these planetary hours? I am not.

Planetary Motions: (see Mean Motions)

Planetary Patterns: (see Configurations)

Planetary Periods: The time it takes for each planet to complete one orbit of the Sun. Of course the Earth takes one year; Mercury takes almost 88 Earth days; Venus takes a bit more than 224 Earth days; Mars takes one year, 10 months, and 21 days; The Asteroids approximately three and one half to four and one half years; Jupiter takes almost 12 years; Saturn takes almost 30 years; Uranus—84 years; Neptune—almost 165 years; and Pluto—more than 247 years.

PLANETS: The planets have been given the names of the mythological gods and goddesses for the simple reason that planet and god represent the same archetype.

Both planets and gods represent the various principles of energy, the many kinds of activity that living creatures experience.

The ramifications of these key words are most astonishingly wide-ranging.

Sun	—identity, will, and purpose
Moon	—emotional responsiveness and instinct
Mercury	—perception
Venus	—completion
Mars	—initiation
Jupiter	—expansion
Saturn	—contraction
Uranus	—individuality

Neptune — conformity
Pluto — obsession

The first four asteroids identify four facets of the feminine principle, fundamental needs which the Moon and Venus do not encompass.

Ceres — food and the labor to produce it

Juno — clothing, the enhancement of life, and atmosphere

Pallas — ingenuity, autonomy, and self-sufficiency

Vesta — shelter, safety, security and belonging

(see individual entries for each planet for fuller description)

PLUTO: Pluto is the most recently discovered planet. He was discovered in February of 1930 by the astronomer Clyde Tombaugh. However, it was Percival Lowell's solution to the problem of a ninth planet that led to the discovery of Pluto. Thus the appropriateness of the joined initials PL for Percival Lowell as the glyph for Pluto.

For most of the 247 years it takes him to complete his orbit of the Sun, Pluto is the most distant planet in the solar system. From his vantage point, the Sun is perceived only as a bright star. Pluto is nearly four billion miles away from the Sun. He really dwells in darkness, in Tartarus, the place of shades and shadows and dank coldness. Pluto's orbit is more highly inclined to the ecliptic than any of the other planets except the asteroid Pallas. It is a very eccentric orbit which brings him inside the orbit of Neptune at perihelion (where he is now and will remain until 1999). In fact, Pluto comes closer to the Sun than Neptune ever does because of his eccentric orbit which is greater than that of Mercury, though not as great as that of Juno. Certain more recent observations of Pluto also suggest that his axis of rotation lies close to the plane of the ecliptic, like that of Uranus.

Pluto is a very small planet, and seems to be growing smaller the more that is discovered about him. At first he was thought to be about the size of Mars, but the most recent measurements show that he is even smaller than our Moon! The moon's diameter is 3476 km. Pluto's is 3000 km. Surprisingly, Pluto is a gaseous body like the four big Jovians; Jupiter, Saturn, Uranus and Neptune; his atmosphere, however, is frozen, and this frozen methane makes him appear to be a hard rocky body like the inner terrestrial planets. Here on earth, methane is a gas created by decayed organic mater.

If one considers the small size of Pluto in conjunction with his vast distance from the Sun, the penchant that many astrologers and researchers have to dismiss the asteroids because they are small doesn't make much sense. Pluto is so far away that if he has the impact of a pebble it's a lot. But this tiny planet is a very powerful principle. The asteroids by comparison are our next door neighbors — only 2.8 Astronomical Units distant from the Sun. Remember, proximity affects the perception of size. For example, our Moon, small though it is, equals the size of the Sun from our perspective, and definitely has a measurable effect on the tides of the earth.

Pluto has a satellite, but one which is relatively quite large and whose orbit is exceedingly close to its parent; together they are more like a double planet. This satellite has been given the name Charon, the ferryman of the River Styx, the poisonous stream in Tartarus.

Mythologically, Pluto is the surly god of the underworld who, as Graves puts it, seldom left Tartarus except on business or when overcome by sudden lust as when he abducted Persephone. The name Plutus means "riches in the earth," the most notorious of which is oil, black gold. But the earth contains many treasures—all the decayed organic matter from sewage, waste, fallen leaves, carrion, sooner or later become nutrients for new life, new growth, and a new source of wealth. Oil is ancient decayed organic matter, transformed through eons of time into precious fuel.

Astrologically, Pluto is the principle of obsession, a phenomenon connected with the concern for survival. Matters that are merely troublesome to most people seem to assume life and death proportions to those who have Pluto or the sign he rules, Scorpio, prominent in their charts. And there are times when the person who is experiencing Pluto transits or progressions behaves like one possessed. Pluto may be obsessive, but he is very creative, richly resourceful, and imaginative in finding solutions to problems or explanations of why things are the way they are, deepening our understanding of matters of life and death.

There is an investigative aspect to Pluto and Scorpio, a desire to get to the bottom of things. It is a wonderful sign and planet for psychologists, doctors, and analysts of all kinds. It is good for research.

Pluto and Scorpio are often emphasized in the horoscopes of politicians, too. Politics requires operating very subtly. It re-

quires secrecy, manipulation, scheming, analysis, planning, and preparation.

Pluto and the sign Scorpio have to do with the part of our bodies which eliminates waste, the large intestine. Survival depends on cleansing our bodies of waste material, which with time and weathering, becomes fertilizer, enriching the earth and providing nutrients for further growth. Recycling is a Pluto-Scorpio phenomenon. In death our very bodies eventually become fertilizer. In a sense, this is what is meant by death and rebirth. Persephone, who was carried off to the underworld by Pluto, was reborn. She comes to life again every spring, when the earth begins to flower once again. She is the death that becomes new life. Persephone represents the transformative, regenerative aspect of Pluto and the sign Scorpio. Robert Graves says that Pluto represents the ineluctability of death, while Persephone represents the hope of rebirth.

There is a connection between the word "death" and "debts." When we die, that which we received from life is returned, paid back. And it seems that indebtedness is a preoccupation with Pluto and the sign Scorpio, too. Indebtedness means being in someone else's power, that someone else has control over our energies. It is a kind of death.

Ponderous Planets: Saturn, Jupiter, and Mars were so called because they move slower than Venus and Mercury. This term was assigned to these bodies before the discovery of Uranus, Neptune, and Pluto, and so undoubtedly these newcomers should be included.

PRECESSION: About 6,000 years ago, the constellation behind the Sun at the time of the vernal equinox was Taurus.

153

That's right, the Sun was entering the *sign Aries, which it does at every vernal equinox, but the constellation behind the Sun was Taurus.* About 2,000 years later, the constellation Aries formed the background of the Sun at the vernal equinox. And so, for a short time, about 2,000 years, both constellation and sign concurred. Then, about 2,000 years after that period, the constellation Pisces began to appear behind the Sun at the vernal equinox. Today, we are nearing the beginning of the constellation Pisces and backing up into the constellation Aquarius which will be the new background to the Sun at the vernal equinox. This slow backward movement of the equinoctial point through the constellations over time, so that at the time of the vernal equinox the background constellation of the Sun gradually changes, is called the precession of the equinoxes. It takes about 26,000 years for the constellations to complete an entire twelvefold precession of the equinoxes. It takes approximately 2,166 years for one constellation to precess backward through the Sidereal Zodiac.

It should be apparent that there are two Zodiacs. The Sidereal Zodiac which contains the constellations found on the Ecliptic, and the Tropical Zodiac which is that initiated when the Sun enters Aries at the time of the vernal equinox. The Tropical Zodiac is the one astrologers use and has nothing whatsoever to do with the Sidereal Zodiac. At least not for interpretation of current, modern-day horoscopes.

Why does this precession occur? The Earth has several movements; it rotates on its axis, it orbits the Sun, and it also does a sort of slow wobble, like a top wobbling as it spins. One rotation of this slow wobble of the earth takes about 26,000 years. It is this wobble that causes the North Pole to point to one or another different Polar Stars over time and also causes the slow shifting backward of the constellations.

What the background constellations show are the Ages of Man: the Gemini Age, which is very likely the period when humankind developed writing; the Taurean Age, which was the period when the pyramids were built, when wealth was first accumulated; the Aries Age, when iron weapons appeared and the age of conquest had arrived, the age of the warrior, the hero; the Pisces Age, when the sacrifice on the cross initiated the Christian era; and now we are headed for a new age, the Age of Aquarius, which, let us hope, will be the age of "The Brotherhood of Humankind." (see Zodiac)

Prediction: Prediction happens in astrology, but never so that one is confident of it before the event. Astrologers can never know, literally, the course that any life will take. They can get some clues and hints of major changes and developments in our lives, and these clues may be useful aids to consciousness, but astrologers can never be totally cognizant of the way in which our lives will unfold. Even if they could predict, their advice could not change the path or course of our development. If an astrologer starts giving you advice, run the other way. Never put the choice of the path you wish to follow into someone else's hands; that choice must always be your own.

Prehistoric Observation: Star-gazing was easy in pre-literate times; there were no city lights to dim the stars. Early humankind looked with awe at the nightly celestial display and discovered the incredible regularity and dependability of the movements of the Sun, Moon, stars, and planets. There is evi-

155

dence of humankind's recognition of the profound importance of the solstices and equinoxes in such early structures as the Pyramids, Stonehenge and the many other places on Earth where markers were set to indicate when the Sun had reached those crucial points in the heavens indicating major seasonal changes. Some of these structures were so sophisticated, they were like giant calculators that even enabled their builders to foretell eclipses. It was probably when agriculture developed in the Neolithic period that humankind realized that in the heavens they had a clock for timing their earthly labors in the fields. The wise men and women in the clans learned they could do even more than that with their astrological observations of the planets' motions. Gradually, astrology emerged.

Primary Directions: This is a method of prediction. It involves much work because the Ecliptic positions given in the ephemeris must be transposed to right ascension. A system used today by few astrologers, but with the advent of computers, the arduous work is eliminated and this system may find favor once again.

Principle Places: These are the five places where the Lights are said to be most efficacious: the tenth, first, seventh, eleventh, and ninth Houses. Nonsense. Wherever your Sun is, it must do the work of that house and you wouldn't have it any other way. The principle place for anything in your chart is exactly where everything is.

PROGRESSIONS: This is a system for moving the planets after birth whereby the timing and nature of any major new development in the person's life may be identified. This system of prediction is sometimes called "secondary directions."

It is based upon the concept that a day's motion of the planets equals a year of life. So, if the Sun, whose motion is about a degree a day were in the fifth degree of Gemini and in 10 days' time would come to a conjunction with a planet in 15 degrees of the same sign, this would indicate that at the age of 10, a major development in the person's life could be expected. The house where this progressed conjunction occurred would tell the circumstance in the life affected, the sign would tell the medium of development, and the planets involved the kind of activity indicated. But not with any literal specificity.

Promittor: A term applied to the planets because in their movement they "prom"ise to fulfill certain indications or portents derived from their radical or birth positions by sign, house, and aspect.

Proper Motion: Refers to the counter-clockwise motion of the planets through the signs.

Prorogator: According to Ptolemy, the name given to a progressing planet when it is about to move into aspect with another planet. No longer in use. (see Ptolemy and Progression)

Psychics: There are people who call themselves astrologers but are not. They are psychics who use astrology as a stimulus of their psychic gifts. Sometimes they are absolutely wonderful. I knew of one who could tell the birth time of a person when it was not known. But often they have an inadequate or overly simplified understanding of the nature of the planets, the signs and the houses. If their psychic gifts are inadequate or inferior, they can do serious damage to their clients and to the reputation of astrology, so beware.

Ptolemy, Claudius: He was the last great Greek astronomer of antiquity. He flourished around 140 AD. He compiled a series of 13 volumes on astronomy known as the Almagest. It is our main source of information about Greek astronomy.

One of Ptolemy's accomplishments was the measurement of the distance to the Moon. He also conceived of a complex system of epicycles to account for the retrograde and direct motion of the planets. It was erroneous, but it worked, and is a tribute to his genius. He is the author of the major aspects between the planets—the Ptolemaic aspects—which are the most widely used by astrologers. (See Aspects.)

Pythagoras: A philosopher—mathematician—astronomer; an Ionian who lived around 500 BC. He believed the Earth, Moon, and planets were round. His concept of the universe was a series of concentric spheres in which each of the seven moving objects—the planets, the Sun, and the Moon—was carried by a separate sphere from the one that carried the stars, so that the motions of the planets resulted from independent rotations of the different spheres about the earth. The friction between them gave rise to harmonious sounds, the "music of the spheres," which only the most gifted ear could hear.

QUADRANTS: The four quarters of the heavens. From 0 Aries to 0 Cancer, from 0 Cancer to 0 Libra, from 0 Libra to 0 Capricorn, and from 0 Capricorn to 0 Aries.

Quadrature: The four signs in the Cardinal Quadrature are Aries, Libra, Cancer, and Capricorn; the four in the Fixed Quadrature are Taurus, Scorpio, Leo, and Aquarius; the four signs in the Mutable Quadrature are Gemini, Virgo, Sagittarius, and Pisces. All of the signs in the Cardinal Quadrature are in square aspect to each other as are those in the Fixed and Mutable Quadratures. (see Signs)

Querent: In horary astrology, when a chart is set up for the answer to a question, the querent is the person who asks the question. The significator of that person is the ruler of the Ascendant, and the co-significator is the Moon.

Radical Elections: These are charts created to ascertain the most auspicious time for beginning any important undertaking, business or otherwise. But instead of setting up the chart for the enterprise, the choice of time is based on the birth chart or the "radix".

Radix: The horoscope of birth, or the foundation horoscope for any business, edifice, etc.

Rapt Motion: The apparent diurnal motion of the heavens caused by the rotation of the Earth on its axis is called rapt motion. A clockwise motion—rising in the east and setting in the west—it is distinguished from proper motion which relates to the counter-clockwise motion of a body through the Zodiac in its orbit or revolution about the Sun.

Rapt Parallels: Those that are formed by the apparent motion of the heavens, and by which two bodies in a sextile relation are carried, or rapt, until they come to equal distances from the Meridian or Horizon.

Rays: In astrology, a planet is under the "rays" of another when within orb of a conjunction or other aspect. This term is no longer used. We simply see if the planet is within orbs of aspect to another planet or one of the lights. (see Aspects)

Reception: When a planet occupies a sign ruled by another planet it is said to be "received" by the latter, as if the first planet were a visitor and the second, a host. If Ceres enters Scorpio, the sign ruled by Pluto, then Ceres is "received" by Pluto. When two planets are in each other's signs they are said to be in "mutual reception." For example, Ceres is the ruler of Virgo. If Pluto were in Virgo when Ceres was in Scorpio the planets would be in mutual reception. This creates a merging of energies—a type of cooperation. It's kind of cute. Just the same, planets must manifest their energies in the medium of the sign they occupy.

RECEPTOR: A term I coined to describe planets or other sensitive points in the horoscopes of individuals, cities, states, organizations, and institutions when they receive an aspect from a transiting planet, from mutual aspects between two or more planets, the degree of a planet's station or a solar or lunar eclipse. (see Aspects, Sensitive Degrees)

Rectification: There are many methods for determining the exact time of birth when it is not known. The inventors of these methods all swear to their accuracy, but I find them all suspect, and no more reliable than the many systems for finding the winner in a horse race. I would rather trust the intuition of a really good psychic who can pick the correct birth time from some invisible clock on the celestial wall.

For heaven's sake, time your babies' births. Write the time down in the baby book along with other vital statistics. In all the years I have been an astrologer I know of only two birth times which I can say are exactly accurate; one is that of my own daughter, for I could see the clock from the delivery table, and the other the baby of an astronomer friend, where the birth was timed to the second.

Refranation: The term used to describe a developing aspect between two planets which never culminates because one of the planets turns retrograde. It "refrains." It signifies that the promised effect will not come to pass. This is something that happens very frequently, but I have never called it "refranation." It is an awkward word. I merely note that it is an aspect that will never happen.

Religion: It was not until I became an astrologer that I realized how deeply religious I am. But I am not loyal to nor do I believe in any man-made religion. I feel awe and profound reverence for the intelligence (or whatever it is) that is behind the incredibly beautiful and orderly working of the universe, the solar system, and the planet which is our home, the dear Earth. How wonderful.

RETROGRADE: The normal direction of movement of the planets is eastward, counter-clockwise. Periodically in their orbits, all of the heavenly bodies except the Sun and Moon appear to cease their normal motion through the signs, to stand still (become stationary) for a time and then begin to move clockwise, to retrace their steps, so to speak, and move back (retrograde) through the sign. After a time, determined by their distance from the Sun, they appear to stop once again (have a station) and return to direct motion.

Of course the planets don't stop moving. That is an illusion created from the perspective of the Earth and the relative motions of Earth and another planet. We can see this phenomenon on Earth if we take a train and encounter another train going in the same direction. Should our train and that other one be moving at the same speed, it will appear that the other train is standing still. Should our train be moving faster, it will appear that the other train is moving backwards (retrograde), and should the other train pick up speed, we will say it has gone Direct again. (see Stations)

These changes in direction do some very interesting things astrologically. For one thing, there will be potential aspects (developments in a person's life) that will never happen because of the change in direction (refranation) and other aspects which have already occurred will by the same token be repeated as the planet moves backward. These stations parallel profound changes in the course of a person's life!

Revolutions: The time in which a planet revolves about the Sun is its heliocentric revolution. The Moon and all of the man-made satellites up there perform a geocentric revolution.

Right Ascension: Angular position measured eastward along the Equator from the first point of Aries; usually measured not in 360 degrees but in 24 hours. Right ascension and declination comprise the equatorial system of mapping the sky and correspond to longitude and latitude on the earth.

Right Distance: The distance from one point to another in right ascension.

Rising Planet: Planets in the twelfth house within five degrees of the Ascendant, or in the first or second houses are said to be "rising." These planets are very important indicators of qualities present in the personality of, or describe matters that are of great personal significance to the native.

Rising Sign: (see Ascendant)

Rotation: From the Latin *rota,* meaning "wheel"; for example, the earth rotates, or spins, around its own axis.

Ruler of Nativity: The ruler of the Rising Sign.

Rulerships: Each sign has a planet which is said to be its ruler, except for Virgo and Libra, which were arbitrarily assigned Mercury and Venus as rulers respectively because the true rulers of these signs had not been discovered. As a matter of fact, before the discovery of Uranus, Neptune, and Pluto, all the planets "ruled" two signs: Mars ruled both Aries and Scorpio; Venus ruled both Taurus and Libra; Mercury ruled both Gemini and Virgo; Jupiter ruled both Sagittarius and Pisces; and Saturn ruled both Capricorn and Aquarius. The Sun and Moon ruled only one sign Each; the Moon—Cancer, and the Sun—Leo.

When Uranus, Neptune, and Pluto came along, they relieved Saturn, Jupiter, and Mars of double duty and gave Aquarius to Uranus, Pisces to Neptune, and Scorpio to Pluto. That still left Mercury and Venus in charge of two signs each. Now, many astrologers who see the sense of having the recently discovered planets ruling Aquarius, Pisces, and Scorpio, still accept the assignment of Mercury ruling Virgo and Venus ruling Libra despite the fact that the asteroids are perfectly suited as the true rulers of these signs.

The ruler of a sign must always have something simpatico with the sign it rules. Thus Aries, the sign of war and conquest is ruled by Mars, the warrior; Taurus, the most sensual

164

pleasure-seeking sign of all, is ruled by Venus, goddess of pleasure and gratification; Gemini, the sign of communication and information, is ruled by Mercury, the storyteller and inventor of the alphabet; Cancer, the emotional water sign, is ruled by the Moon, she who rules the tides of the oceans; Leo, the sign of pride, power, and identity is ruled by the supreme power of our solar power system, the Sun; Virgo, the sign of productivity and harvest is ruled by the productive goddess of the grain and the harvest, Ceres, and perhaps also by Vesta; and Libra, the sign of justice and relationship, is ruled by Juno, the goddess of marriage and childbirth, and by Pallas, the goddess of wisdom and justice; Scorpio, the sign of death and rebirth, is ruled by Pluto, the god of the underworld; Sagittarius, the enthusiastic sign of administration, is ruled by Jupiter, the big, bombastic wheeler-dealer in the heavens; Capricorn, the sign of reality, structuring, and building, is ruled by old Saturn, the planet of crystallization, form, sensitivity, and depth (reality); Aquarius, the sign of the brotherhood of man that accepts the individual differences between people, is ruled by Uranus, the planet of freedom, independence, and individuality; and Pisces, the sign of compassion, empathy, and self-giving is ruled by Neptune, the principle of conformity, of egolessness, and self-losing.

Ruminant Signs: This refers to the signs Aries, Taurus, and Capricorn. Do these natives ruminate? Do they chew the cud? I doubt it, though Taurus mulls things over a lot.

SAGITTARIUS: It is a Mutable Fire sign; therefore it describes the psychological function Centroverted Feeling-Sensation.

This is the ninth sign of the Zodiac. It comes in the third month of the fall season. Why does this, a Fire sign, appear at the time of the year when it is growing cold, when winter is almost upon us? Well, even in cold weather, one must keep warm. How do we do it? We build fires, we pile on clothing for insulation, we turn up the thermostat, we stay indoors as much as possible — find some cozy nook to hibernate in if we are a bear — in which case we will have put on considerable fat as fuel to sustain us through the winter, or we keep busy, generating heat through activity. We go hunting, ice skating, skiing, have snowball fights, or we travel to a warmer climate; we migrate. Like the birds, we go on a distant journey, only we hop a plane or board a train.

I do believe that many Sagittarian traits have grown out of the need to keep warm in the short days and long nights when fall turns into winter.

The Fire signs express the psychological function feeling. And it is true that the great urge in Sagittarius is to share feelings, to share enthusiasms with others. It is like Rah! Rah! Rah! in the football stadium, or Ole! in the arena. All of those voices united in support of their team, or the toreador fighting the poor, disadvantaged, but brave bull; all sharing their enthusiasm with each other. This sign is much associated with sports, especially team sports, but really with any sport. Originally, I suspect the activity where team enthusiasm first arose was in the prehistoric hunt, a very masculine activity. Nowadays, this team spirit shows up in men's clubs, stag parties, and in the business world, where sales people are revved up with enthusiasm for their product in preparation for "making a killing" in the business world.

Sagittarius is not only associated with sports, it is one of the business signs. Marc Jones called this the sign of administration, and indeed these people are often very gifted with administrative skills, with the ability to organize, to manage, to delegate responsibility, and to direct the action. They can arouse enthusiasm in their associates about any projects in which they may be involved, not only in business. Although not necessarily the Sun sign, Sagittarius may be rising or contain an unusual concentration of planets in the charts of managers, directors, conductors, and administrative producers in various fields such as music, film, and dance. Broadcasting, publishing, and the travel industry also figure prominently with this sign.

Sagittarius is ruled by the giant of planets, Jupiter, often called the Striped Giant for the encircling bands of color and spots of red and white on his surface. Curiously, many Sagittarians seem to be very partial to stripes and spots in fashion, clothing, decor. Stripes are associated with the racetrack tout as well as with the business person.

It is a fact that Sagittarians tend to be tall, long-legged, and to walk a lot; they tend to put on weight, especially around the hams and thighs (protection against the cold and scarcity of food?). But occasionally one encounters a diminutive Sagittarian, who, though small in stature, is very big in feeling, enthusiasm, and spirit.

Satellites: These are the Moons of the planets; the single Moon of earth, the pair of moons of Mars, and the numerous moons of the planets beyond Mars. Satellites in modern times are also the many man-made Earth-orbiting objects now cluttering up the outer space surrounding the Earth; the tiny artificial moons of Earth.

Satellitium: Another word for Stellium. Three or more planets in the same sign, not necessarily including the Sun, Mercury, and Venus, which are usually very close to each other. Occasionally there may be six, seven, eight, or even more planets in the same sign. People born with such a configuration, especially if the planets are close together, will find that it never rains but pours again and again in their lives, for a transiting planet will shift from contact or aspect to one after another of these planets in conjunction. When there are many planets in the same sign, that sign is being strongly emphasized, and the gifts, talents, virtues, and faults of that particular medium will find continued and repeated expression. A Satellitium may span or reach over into a second sign.

SATURN: The furthermost of the truly visible planets in the solar system. Because he was thought to be the last of the family of planets in our solar system, Saturn is the planet that is associated with limits, the outer limits, the furthest extent, and with time, timing, and old age. The Grim Reaper.

Saturn is a giant, a partner to Jupiter, but not nearly so massive. Like Jupiter, Saturn rotates rapidly on his axis—about 10 and one half hours per rotation. He completes his orbit in 29 and one half years. Saturn's equator is inclined to the ecliptic 27 degrees. This means that unlike Jupiter, Saturn has seasons.

Saturn is most famous for his magnificent ring system. We now know that all of the giant planets have ring systems, but none of the others is so flamboyantly gorgeous as Saturn's. That ring system is composed of billions of chunks of water ice, or rocks of various sizes coated with ice, that glitter and glisten, reflecting sunlight. They orbit the planet at its equator in a very thin plane.

Another very interesting peculiarity about Saturn is the fact that this is a very light planet, the least dense of all the planets. Saturn is no more dense than ordinary hardwood. If we could get a piece of Saturn here on Earth it would float in water. And this is curious because the metal associated with Saturn is lead, a very heavy element.

Physical facts have symbolic import, so what can we make of these facts about the planet Saturn?

The ring system: It is thought that at one time, long ago, the bits of rocks and ice orbiting Saturn were scattered about, randomly orbiting the planet. But that as time passed, this gi-

169

ant body gradually caused them to settle down into the neat, thin, and orderly plane where we now find them. Since Saturn is seen by many to be stern taskmaster and disciplinarian, perhaps this ordering of the rings symbolizes that aspect of Saturn. Saturn organized the rings, structured them, and put them in their place.

Saturn is ruler of the sign Capricorn, the Cardinal Earth Sign, the first month of winter. Capricorn is the exact opposite, the antithesis of the summer Water Sign Cancer, the sign of flowing water. In this winter sign, water freezes, it crystallizes, it has form, it does not flow. The rings of Saturn, composed as they are of ice and rocks, are suggestive of these very important aspects of Saturn; structure and form, and crystallization. Saturn gives form to things. On Earth we know that Saturn is involved with the structure of things, with the skeleton, the bones, the teeth, with rocks, and with mountains. Cardinal Earth is mountain country—not flat plains or rolling hills. So Capricorn and Saturn be involved in mountain building. Mountains, the habitat of the frolicsome, sure-footed, beautiful mountain goat, which is Capricorn's symbol.

As for the lightness, the lack of density of this planet: could it be the symbolic indicator of the sensitivity of Saturn and the sign Capricorn? Saturn and Capricorn rule not only the bony structure, the form of things, but the skin, our main sensory organ—sensation, a very important function if one wants to be in touch with reality. Having been trained in the school of "hard knocks," Saturn is sensitive to being hurt; his lack of density may symbolize oversensitivity, shyness, vulnerability, fearfulness, and a keen awareness of physical reality.

Mythologically, Saturn is the father of six great gods and goddesses Vesta, Ceres, Juno, Pluto, Neptune, and Jupiter. It was prophesied by Mother Earth that one of his sons would dethrone him, therefore he devoured each child at birth. When Jupiter, the sixth child, was born, Rhea, the long-suffering mother of this brood, gave her rather slow-witted consort a stone wrapped in swaddling clothes to swallow. The trick worked and she was able to hide Jupiter safely away. When Jupiter was ready to take over, he gave Saturn a potion to drink which caused him to regurgitate the swallowed sisters and brothers, and his grateful siblings asked Jupiter to lead them in a war against the Titans which lasted 10 years. In the end the brothers and their allies were victorious. They then shook lots in a helmet for the lordship of the sky, sea and murky underworld. Jupiter won the sky, Neptune the sea and Pluto the underworld.

When Galileo first looked at Saturn through the primitive telescope he created, he is said to have exclaimed "Saturn does indeed devour his children." For what he thought he saw through his telescope was a globe at the sides of which were attached two smaller objects which gradually disappeared. What he really saw were the rings and which gradually disappeared as time passed due to the changing angle of our earthly perspective of the planet and its rings.

Scales, The: The emblem associated with the sign Libra. Justice holding a scale. She is blind, and weighs the evidence with utterly impartial judgment.

SCORPIO: The eighth sign of the Zodiac. The Fixed sign in the Water triplicity. Since Fixed signs manifest in an introverted mode and Water expresses intuition, the sign Scorpio represents the psychological function Introverted—Intuition.

This sign appears in the second month of the fall season. What is happening in the Earth at that time of year? This is probably the gloomiest month, even more melancholy than December or January. At least with the Sun's entry into Sagittarius and Capricorn, the holiday season has arrived, and there is a sense of optimism and hope; there will be feasting, partying, and merrymaking. But while the Sun is in Scorpio there is a moodiness, a gloominess, a foreboding of death and decay. The days are growing shorter, frost is in the air, and skies are often broodingly gray and dismal, the fallen leaves are rotting on the ground, the growing season has ended in most northern latitude places, and, until the last century, man was compelled to hunt and kill in order to survive. Small wonder that this sign is called the sign of death. But it is from the very death and decay that surrounds us in the heart of autumn that new life will arise when spring returns.

I believe that in earlier eras late fall brought a recognition of mortality. Survival was a touchy proposition, compelling humankind to tap inner, hidden resources of creativity in order to make it through the dark night of the coming winter. And so Scorpio is not only a sign of awareness of death, but is also associated with survival and rebirth. It is the sign of creativity, of the capacity to tap the inner creative resources of the human psyche.

Scorpio is the most intense, analytical, investigative, probing, digging, wanting-to-get-to-the-bottom-of-things, of all the signs. It is not content with any merely superficial explanation of actions, events, or circumstances. Those people with the Sun, Moon, or an unusual concentration of planets in this Sign must make their own way in the world, must put their own mark or stamp upon whatever they touch, will not have the evaluations or judgments of others imposed upon them. They know for sure when there is more there than meets the eye and will not be content until they have unearthed it. Sometimes they are like a voice crying in the wilderness. They know something, they try to tell it, but nobody seems to understand the vision they are trying with meager success to communicate.

There is something very disturbing to others about the natives of the sign Scorpio. They can make other people feel they are being seen through (and indeed they often are), which creates an uneasiness, a discomfort. Their intuition is always at work probing the surface appearance of things, piercing the facade of human pretensions. They are often attracted to psychotherapy, psychoanalysis, and also to politics.

This is a very rationalizing sign. It is inclined to great secrecy, but there are times when it can be exceedingly and courageously honest, and can appear to be cruel in its willingness to articulate difficult truths. Scorpio can dish it out, but it can also take it. In fact, because of the capacity to "take it" and survive, it is inclined to expect others less sturdy and resilient to be able to do the same.

Secondary Directions: (see Progressions)

Semi-arc: Half an arc, or the time that a planet takes to come from the Horizon to the Midheaven, or from the Midheaven to the Horizon. This is the diurnal semi-arc. The opposite of this, from the Horizon to the Nadir or from the Nadir to the

Horizon, is the nocturnal semi-arc. It may be expressed in degrees and minutes of a circle, or in hours and minutes.

SENSITIVE DEGREES: Certain degrees of the Zodiac where planets have had either Retrograde or Direct stations or where solar or lunar eclipses have occurred. These degrees are imprinted with or sensitized in the nature of the heavenly bodies that have had the stations or eclipses for varying lengths of time—as much as two years for a Direct Station of Mars and one and one half years for a Direct Station of Venus. Thus an effect is felt long after the planet has moved away from the degree where it had the station. When other transiting planets make aspects to the sensitive degree an effect will be felt that reflects the natures of the aspecting planet and the planet that had the station filtered through the medium of the signs involved.

Those aspects made to sensitive degrees are called Hidden Aspects, for it is not immediately apparent that an aspect has occurred; there is no planet there. Nevertheless, these Sensitive Degrees are extremely potent and their effectiveness can be demonstrated in their manifest effect in the world. The planet or point in the birth charts that responds to these Sensitive Degrees are called Receptors.

Separation: When two bodies have been in exact aspect, and are separating from each other. The aspect has culminated and the development indicated by the aspect has peaked and is now beginning to subside.

Sidereal Astrology: Sidereal means pertaining to the stars or constellations; astral. Sidereal astrology is a system of astrology that is based on the actual star constellations, the star formations of the original Zodiac. In the early centuries when astrology was first becoming established, it was not realized that the equinoxes precessed backwards through the heavens, causing a gradual change in the constellation behind the sun at the vernal equinox. It is this original Zodiac that sidereal astrologers use. They do not give credence to the Tropical Zodiac which is initiated at the vernal equinox.

The Tropical Zodiac, which most astrologers use, is separate and distinct from the actual constellations. The first sign, Aries, is initiated when the Ecliptic and Equator intersect at the vernal equinox. The first day of spring is when we say the Sun has entered 0 Aries, but the actual constellation behind the Sun may be any one of the 12 constellations in the 26,000 years it takes for a complete cycle of precession to occur. At one time more than four thousand years ago, the first point of Aries did coincide with the sidereal constellation of Aries, and will again, but not for many thousands of years to come.

As for sidereal astrology, its practitioners cannot make much use of the signs, for in that system they overlap each other and clear definitions are not possible. But they do use the aspects, the contacts between the planets, and this apparently gives them enough credibility to enable them to survive.

Sidereal Zodiac: The star groupings, the original constellations which are found on the ecliptic, on the Sun's path in his journey through the signs, or on the earth's path in its journey around the Sun.

SIGNS:

Positive or Masculine signs: Rational, Judgmental
Aries, Gemini, Leo, Libra, Sagittarius, and Aquarius

QUADRATURES

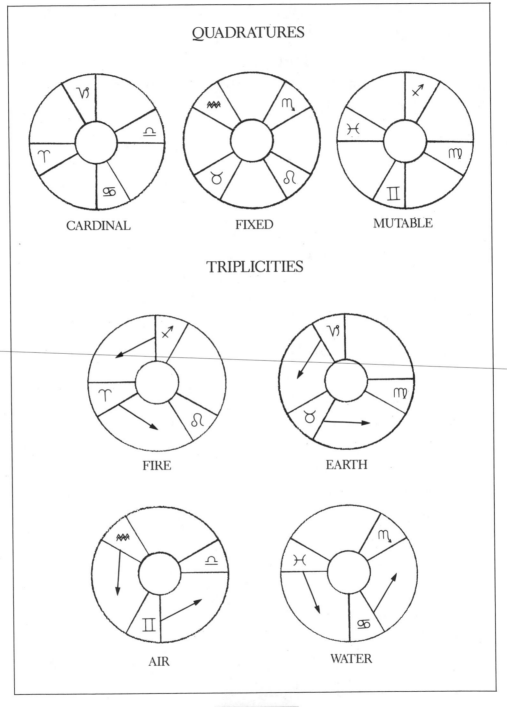

CARDINAL   FIXED   MUTABLE

TRIPLICITIES

FIRE   EARTH

AIR   WATER

Negative or Feminine signs: Non-rational, Perceptive
Taurus, Cancer, Virgo, Scorpio, Capricorn, and Pisces
Signs, Light and Dark: (Please take the following asser-
tions with a grain of salt. I record them only because
they appear in the old astrology books.) The first half
of all positive signs denotes light complexions. The latter
half of the same signs shows dark complexions. Similarly the first half of negative signs shows dark complexions, while the latter half indicates light complexions.

Quadratures: General Attitude

	Cardinal (Extrovert)	Fixed (Introvert)	Mutable (Centrovert)
Spring	Aries	Taurus	Gemini
Summer	Cancer	Leo	Virgo
Fall	Libra	Scorpio	Sagittarius
Winter	Capricorn	Aquarius	Pisces

Triplicities: Elements, Functions

	Fire (Feeling)	Air (Thinking)	Earth (Sensation)	Water (Intuition)
Cardinal:	Aries	Libra	Capricorn	Cancer
Fixed:	Leo	Aquarius	Taurus	Scorpio
Mutable:	Sagittarius	Gemini	Virgo	Pisces

Signs of Long Ascension: Long ascension means that it takes
a greater amount of time for the thirty degrees of these signs
to come up over the horizon. If the average movement of a
sign as it rises above the horizon takes two hours, signs of long
ascension would take perhaps two and one half hours. In northern latitudes the signs of long ascension are Cancer, Leo, Vir-

go, Libra, Scorpio and Sagittarius.

The significance of the above is that more people are born with signs of long ascension rising than with signs of short ascension rising. This is of interest to statisticians who are concerned about demographics in establishing statistical norms.

Signs of Short Ascension: Short ascension means that it will take less than two hours for the sign to move completely above the horizon, less time than it takes the signs of long ascension. The signs of short ascension in the northern latitudes are Capricorn, Aquarius, Pisces, Taurus, and Gemini. Fewer people are born with one or another of these signs rising.

In southern latitudes the signs of long and short ascension are reversed.

Signs of Voice (or Speaking Signs): These are the "Human" Signs: Gemini, Virgo, Libra, and Aquarius. These are the signs which express the psychological function of thinking.

Sinister Aspects: (see Aspects)

Slow of Course: When a planet moves slower than its mean motion it is said to be slow of course. I believe the slower a planet moves, which is what happens when a planet is getting ready for a Retrograde or Direct station, the greater is its impact. It stays in contact with or aspect to a planet in the birthchart for a longer time, intensifying and extending the duration of its effect. If a person is born with a slow-moving planet or stationary planet in his birth chart, the significance of that principle in the person's life is greatly enhanced.

Sol: The Sun, Helios, Apollo.

Solstices: When the Sun enters zero Cancer and zero Capricorn; the summer and winter solstices. The two instances

in the year when the Sun is farthest north of the celestial Equator (June) and farthest south of it (December). These are times when the Sun is stationary, stops its climb or its decline, and changes direction. At the summer solstice we experience the longest day, and at the winter solstice the longest night.

Southern Hemisphere Astrology: Although the seasons are reversed in southern latitude countries, it is a curious fact that a northern latitude interpretation of the signs prevails. Australian astrologers confirm this for us. Psychologically, the sign Aries retains its springtime spirit in those places, even though the actual season they are experiencing is fall. So it is with all of the signs. I believe that the reason for this is that consciousness was originally imprinted with a northern latitude orientation, many millions of years ago—the original seasonal DNA so to speak. Then, as the races evolved, and humankind and other creatures emigrated or migrated to farther southern or farther northern latitudes, they carried with them that original imprint. Only a small part of Africa, and South America, Australia, and New Zealand actually are below the Equator.

Southern Signs: The signs from Libra to Pisces are called southern signs, for in the mundane horoscope with Aries rising, these signs would be above the Horizon, and therefore south. South is overhead; north is below the Horizon.

Sowing by the Moon: Many *Old Farmer's Almanacs* contain much information and advice about astrological conditions favorable for producing a plentiful harvest. The Moon, which has to do with moisture, so necessary to growth and fruitfulness, plays a major part. From an old *Old Farmer's Almanac:* "The best time to plant flowers and vegetables that bear crops above the ground is during the Light of the Moon; that is, between the day the Moon is New to the day it if Full (increasing in light). Flowering bulbs and vegetables that bear crops below ground should be planted during the dark of the Moon, that is from the day after it is Full to the day before it is New again (decreasing in light)."

Gardeners who use the Moon's sign follow these rules: 1) Plant when the Moon is in a fruitful feminine sign—Cancer, Scorpio, Pisces, Taurus, or Capricorn. 2) Cultivate when the Moon is in a barren, masculine sign: Aries, Leo, Virgo, Sagittarius, Gemini, Libra, and Aquarius. (I don't think Virgo belongs in the latter list because it is a feminine sign and comes in the harvest month. Although it may mark the end of the growing season it is the time when seeds are gathered which will be productive of new growth in future years.)

There are specific activities best performed when the Moon is in a certain sign:

Aries: cultivating, plowing, tilling
Taurus: potatoes, root crops, lettuce, cabbage
Gemini: weeding, cultivating, destroying growths
Cancer: best sign for all planting and irrigating
Leo: use only for killing weeds
Virgo: good for cultivation
Libra: planting flowers, seeding hay, and livestock feed
Scorpio: very productive for all planting, especially vines
Sagittarius: cultivation, planting onions, seeding hay
Capricorn: potatoes, root crops, tubers
Aquarius: weeding, destroying pests
Pisces: highly productive, especially for root growing.

Spica Virginis: The star Arista in almost the 24th degree of Libra, near the Ecliptic. It is said to be the most fortunate of all the stars, whatever that means.

Stars: All of the brightest magnitude stars are thought to have some specific significance. Some astrologers are making studies to try to determine the nature of that significance, but at present there is no reliable report on these studies.

Stations, Stationary: The normal movement of the planets in their orbits is counter-clockwise through the Zodiac. All of the planets (except the Sun and Moon) at certain points in their orbits appear to stop moving and stand still: to be stationary. When they start moving again they move backward—clockwise—or as astrologers say, Retrograde. They retrace their steps for a time, after which each planet will "station" once again and resume normal counter-clockwise motion, or "go Direct." We say they are "Stationary Retrograde" or "Stationary Direct."

The period of immobility varies with each planet. Pluto will stay in the same degree and minute for about 15 days, Neptune for 12 days, Uranus for nine days, Saturn for five, Jupiter for four, the asteroids for three, Mars for two, Venus for one and Mercury for less than one day.

It is only in the last few years that astrologers have begun to appreciate the immense significance of these stations. For further information see my book *A Graphic Ephemeris of Sensitive Degrees.* (see Retrograde, Sensitive Degrees.)

Statistics: The statisticians have invaded the world of astrology, and in keeping with their talent for demonstrating that black is white, they have for the most part succeeded in proving that astrology does not work. But statisticians are not astrologers and do not appreciate the complexity of astrological interpretation: they propound overly simplistic tests, or have an inadequate understanding of the factors of astrological interpretation.

One problem statisticians have with regard to astrology is that they want to establish a causal connection to account for astrological phenomena; they want to see some tangible, measurable force, like the gravitational pull of the Moon on the Earth's waters, as evidence of the "influence" of the planets. I know of one statistician who utterly dismisses Mercury, the asteroids, and Pluto as having no astrological significance, simply because they are so small. Any practicing astrologer *knows* better. I prefer Jung's "synchronicity" as a more valid explanation of astrological phenomena.

Sooner or later certain astrology-wise statisticians will find corroborating evidence in their tests which will validate astrology to the satisfaction of even the most hard-nosed non-believer. (see Synchronicity)

Stellium: (see Satellitium)

Stonehenge: A late Stone Age structure in southern England, probably used to mark the timing of the solstices and equinoxes. It had an astronomical-religious function, no doubt.

Storms: One of the asteroids, Juno is a remarkably dependable indicator of important storms, such as tornadoes, hurricanes, and typhoons. Mythologically, she is a "stormy" goddess, and according to Graves, "the winds were originally the property of Hera (Juno) and the male gods had no power over them." Astrology finds her power over the winds to be intact as ever it was.

Strong Signs: The Fixed Signs, because of their frequently conspicuous rigidity and stubborness, may appear to be strong. We know that that is not necessarily the case. There certainly is greater staying power, willfulness, and determination in these signs.

Succedent Houses: (see House Categories)

Sun: Our star: The Prime Mover. In astrology, the indicator of self, will, purpose, and drive. In space larger bodies have a greater gravitational effect on smaller bodies. Although Jupiter is so big that all the planets would fit into it one and one half times, all the planets, including Jupiter, equal only about one percent of the mass of the Sun, if that much. If the Earth were the size of a ping pong ball, the Sun would be a globe nine feet in diameter. Now that's power. Every body in space obeys the Sun, every planet, every comet, every asteroid. All aspects between the planets are mediated through the Sun.

The Sun is, of course, the source of all life on Earth. It warms the Earth, greens it, lights it, and colors it. Small wonder that in many cultures the Sun is the main symbol for God, or is the most powerful aspect of the masculine side of the godhead (as the Moon is the prime indicator of the feminine side of the godhead). But the Sun can be a killer, too. If the greenhouse effect, which is the reason why Venus is such a broiling inferno, gets a foothold here, the mighty energy of the Sun's rays will accumulate and make life unbearable. Or if the shielding ozone layer in our atmosphere is destroyed, many species of life will be destroyed, affecting the food chain. Humans will be vulnerable to skin cancer, and the unmodified, unfiltered energy of the Sun's rays will destroy us. We cannot look directly at his face, nor tolerate his rays without proper shielding.

We have to be very respectful of the Sun. He is the source of everlasting, pure, non-polluting energy, the energy we must learn to tap if our most beautiful but fragile planet is to survive.

Apollo is the Sun God. His arrows represent the radiant energy of the Sun as Diana's arrows represent moonlight. Of course, the Sun is associated with happiness and joy. The birds sing when his light begins to appear in the heavens at dawn. Certain Indians and other primitive peoples, mimicking the birds, sing or make music to welcome his daily appearance or perhaps to magically assure that he will rise.

The Sun is a very dramatic place. A group of astronomers were once watching one of the first films taken of the Sun. Its fire, its huge turbulent sprays of arching flames reaching unimaginable distances above its surface, churning, writhing, glowing . . . it was an amazing thing to see. When it was over, the astronomers all rose and applauded! They couldn't help it; they were overwhelmed. They applauded the *performance* of the Sun.

As indicator of self, the Sun and Leo, the sign he rules, have much to do with identity, with self-discovery, self-expression, and projecting the self. For if the Sun does nothing else, he projects and radiates energy. Self-discovery and self-expression are fun; they delight us. Playing is self-discovery. When little children play at being ballet dancers, astronauts, firefighters, or doctors, they are practicing for adulthood. They are studying. They are, in a way, in school. Astrology wisely points out that learning is a by-product of playing. Through play we experiment with different costumes until we find the one that suits us best. Thus the association of the Sun with the fifth sign and the fifth house, which have to do with fun and games, school, learning, playing, self-expression and self-discovery.

Sun-Sign Astrology: This is the kind of astrology that requires only the date of birth, which yields the sign and the degree of the Zodiac that the Sun was in on the birthday. It is extremely limited and overly general. The location of the Sun is meaningful, and has a significance which will be recognized by the individual, but it is only one aspect of the complex of energies that comprise any person, and often is not the most significant one.

It is this kind of astrology that most frequently appears in newspapers and magazines. Since genuine astrology requires not only the location and date, but the time of birth as well, in order to be specific, merely knowing the location of the Sun is a paltry drop in the bucket in the analysis of a horoscope. Therefore we do not blame the critics of astrology for finding fault with it. If this is their only contact with astrology, they cannot be blamed for rejecting the practice; all serious astrologers do, too.

Sunspots: Dark spots on the Sun, occasionally large enough to be perceived by the naked eye (well-protected by a shielding material of some kind, of course). Astronomically it is now known that the spots that may be seen on the Sun are regions where the gases are cooler than those of the surrounding regions. There are cycles of sunspots, with the maximum and minimum numbers of them changing periodically. The maximum number of sunspots seems to occur at an average inter-

185

val of 11.1 years. Many astrologers believe planetary positions are in some way related to sunspot activity.

Superior Planets: A superior planet is any planet whose orbit is larger than that of Earth, such as Mars, most of the asteroids, Jupiter, Saturn, etc. (see Inferior Planets)

Sweet Signs: The Air Signs. The thinking signs: because thinking means reasoning, which means understanding, which is sweet.

Swift in Motion: When planets are moving at considerably better than mean motion they are said to be swift in motion. The faster a planet moves, the shorter duration in time is its effect.

Symbolism: Astrology is filled with symbolism. The physical, astronomical facts with regard to the planets in the solar system become symbolic of the meaning and nature of the principle that the planets represent. The mythological gods are symbolic of the constellations of energy that the planets which bear their names represent. The glyphs used for the planets and signs are tokens, symbols, shorthand, or hieroglyphics which represent the signs, planets, and gods.

Sympathetic Signs: Signs that are in the same element are in sympathetic stance with each other; the three Fire signs, the three Earth signs, the three Water signs, and the three Air signs.

The so-called feminine Water and Earth signs are in sympathetic stance with each other. The so-called masculine signs are in cooperative stance with each other; Fire and Air signs. These Signs are either in trine or sextile relationship to each other.

Synastry: This is the study of relationship. There are at least two approaches to the study of relationship. One is chart comparison, in which the planets in the chart of one person are placed in the houses of the other, and any aspects between the two charts are studied and analyzed, and vice versa. The other is a very strange and rather recent development: composite charts in which a midpoint is found between the planets of both charts—between the two Suns, the two Moons, the two Mercurys, etc.—and a separate chart is set up using the midpoint between the two Midheavens based on a selected latitude.

Synchronicity: This is a term coined by Carl Gustav Jung to describe what he called "an acausal connecting principle" to account for psychic phenomena, or remarkable coincidences. Astrology may be called an example of synchronicity. The expression "as above, so below," suggests the connection between astronomical phenomena which occur in parallel with human and earthly events *but do not cause them.* When we look at our horoscope, it is as if we are looking into a mirror. We are looking at our reflection, at a pattern, an imprint which was present in the heavens at our birth, but which does not cause us. This heavenly pattern is the macrocosm of our microcosm. In a sense this very individualistic pattern of the planets and the signs they were in at birth is our DNA, the pattern of our basic structure that is present in every cell in our body. But because we can construct a chart of that pattern in the heavens, we can study and analyze the individual it represents. And because it is not static, but moves in time, we can also determine the course of our development, not in any specific manner, but well enough to identify the major developments. For just as the planets keep moving after birth, so we grow and develop, and the changing heavenly pattern reveals that, too.

Synodic: This refers to the period of time it takes for a body to return to the same place in its orbit as seen from the moving earth. For the Moon to complete a revolution with respect to the Sun takes an average of 29 days, 12 hours, 44 minutes, and 2.8 seconds. It is the period from New Moon to New Moon.

This is in contrast to the Moon's revolution with respect to the stars—its sidereal revolution—which is 27 days, seven hours, 43 minutes, and 11.5 seconds.

Synthesis: The putting together of parts so as to form a whole. In astrology, the effort to unify the many factors of the horoscope so as to get a representative picture of the person or the event that the astrological components describe. Synthesis is another word for chart interpretation or analysis.

Syzyges: The conjunction or opposition of the Sun and Moon. New and Full moons. This term may also be applied to the conjunction or opposition of any two celestial bodies.

Tables of Houses: These are the tables showing the degrees of the various signs of the Zodiac occupying the cusps of the houses in any latitude under a given meridian of right ascension or sidereal time. There are several systems of house division, one or another favored by various astrologers: the Alcabitius, Placidus, Campanus, Regiomontanus, and Koch house cusp systems, to mention a few. For each of these one needs appropriate tables of houses. Sets of these tables of houses are available in the astrology bookstores, and if one has a computer, most astrological programs allow the option of selecting the preferred system. The Placidus system is most favored in the United States. Europeans seem to prefer the Campanus system, and recently the Koch system has been climbing in popularity.

TAURUS: Taurus is the second sign of the spring season. It is the Fixed sign in the Earth group, and so it represents the psychological function Introverted Sensation. This is the most intensely sensual of all the signs, and people born with the Sun,

Moon, or an unusual concentration of planets in this sign are extremely sensitive to color, texture, sound, flavor, and scent. These people really rejoice in the creature comforts of life: they have rich taste. One often finds artists, especially painters and singers, to have an emphasis here.

This is the beautiful month. The Earth is in full flower. Meadows and pastures are lush and verdant, and grazing creatures are in their heaven. Ferdinand the bull, the animal associated with this sign, is sniffing the flowers, fattening up on the green of the Earth, and dreaming of romance. It is a fact that the birthday of the stock market is May, when the Sun is in Taurus. Owning livestock or cattle was a mark of wealth in agricultural communities, and still is in many places. We associate the bull with the stock market, and Venus with the bull, for she is the ruler of Taurus, and Venus is the principle of money.

Both Taurus and Venus have to do with money, and Taureans or those with an emphasis of planets in Taurus seem to have a knack for getting value for their money. They are great bargain finders. There are many bankers or money managers found to be associated with this sign.

Integrity is very important to these people and if ever their integrity is questioned, there is a tightening-up, a clamping-down in the throat, and they become almost inarticulate. They withdraw and pull down the curtain.

As with all fixed signs, Taureans are stubborn and inflexible; they're slow to change, tenacious, and reluctant to let go, but once they do, there is no going back. They have great staying power, and once committed to a project will hang in there, follow through, and bring it to completion. These earthy people are attracted to both art and the study of physics.

Temperament: There is a natural disposition inherent in each sign. Probably the temperament associated with the Rising Sign, or Ascendant, is most influential.

Terrestrial: Of the Earth, as opposed to celestial. The terrestrial planets are the Earth, and the other small, hard planets — Mercury, Venus, Mars, as well as the Moon — as opposed to the large, fluid Jovian ones.

Time Differences: Time throughout the world is calculated from midnight or noon in Greenwich, England. Places to the west of Greenwich or in west longitude are earlier in time than in Greenwich. Places to the east of Greenwich are later than the time of Greenwich.

Time Zones: With the development of the railroad and telegraph, it became necessary to standardize time so that people would know when trains would arrive or depart and the correct date and time of the sending and receiving of messages. Before this, people used only local time; sundial time. But with standardization, large areas of land were required to have the same clock time, even though the actual time could vary. Time zones were created approximately every 15 degrees of longitude around the Earth.

The United States has four major time zones not including Alaska and Hawaii: Eastern Standard Time (EST), defined by the 75 degree west meridian (longitude west of Greenwich); Central Standard Time (CST), defined by the 90 degree west meridian; Mountain Standard Time (MST), defined by the 105 degree west meridian; and Pacific Standard Time (PST), defined by the 120 degree west meridian. Hawaii and Alaska both keep the time of the 150 degree west meridian.

All places about seven and one half degrees on either side of the time zone meridians have the same clock time, but there are areas of the globe where there are great deviations from these standards. Another complication has been the introduction in some countries of Daylight Saving Time, which sets the clocks back one hour. And in the event of war, there is War Time, which is the same as Daylight Saving time, and in some places may coincide with it or even be combined with it, to further complicate matters. For astrologers who need the correct birth time, the uncertainties about the time used in certain countries, states, or in different years are a big headache.

TRANSITS: The current movement of the planets in their orbits around the Sun. When a planet enters a sign, we say it is "transiting" through Aries, Taurus, or whatever. When a planet is in a part of the Zodiac wherein we have a planet we say it is "transiting over my Venus, Mars, Ceres," etc. When a transiting planet makes an aspect to another transiting planet, we note the nature of the aspect and the degree of the Zodiac where the aspect occurs to see if it is in aspect to any planet or Sensitive Degree in our own chart or in the charts or horoscopes on which we are working.

Translation of Light: Planets are said to be in aspect to each other when they are within whatever "orb" or degree allowance we accept as our standard. If we say that a planet within 10 degrees of exactitude is making a square to another planet, and 10 degrees is the orb allowance to which we adhere, then an aspect of 11 degrees is out of orb; is too wide to be effective.

So, when one planet, let's say in 12 degrees of Libra, makes a square aspect to a planet in 7 degrees of Capricorn, it will also be in square aspect to a planet in 19 degrees of Cancer. Although the other two planets—the one in 7 degrees of Capricorn and the one in 19 degrees of Cancer—are out of orb with each other, they are brought into aspect by "translation of light," for the planet that aspects both bodies links them.

Transpluto: Many astrologers believe that there is a ninth planet which they call Transpluto. I do not believe that this is the case. Some years ago, a satellite called IRAS was put into orbit. It was a kind of infrared telescope which for many months scoured the heavens, making some phenomenal astronomical discoveries and accumulating data which has yet to be analyzed. But no one has come upon any evidence that there is a 10th planet, although when most astronomers look at this IRAS information, they are primarily interested in finding a planet. New telescopes are being constructed and sent into space to search. Perhaps one of them will find another planet after all.

Trigonometry: A mathematical technique which was at one time essential for astrologers to know in order to calculate the positions of the planets at birth. It is the process of measuring triangles by the use of logarithms. The logarithms of quantities to be multiplied are merely added together and the resulting logarithm gives the answer. Similarly, the logarithms of quantities to be divided are subtracted from one another, and the remainder gives the answer. This is an enormous saving of work. Logarithms are the invention of Baron Napier of Merchiston, who used them to facilitate his astrological calculations. They were originally engraved on ivory tablets and the expression "Napier's Bones" came into use as a popular description of them.

Triplicity: Three signs of the same element, for example; Cancer, Scorpio, and Pisces are members of the water triplicity. (see Signs)

Tropical Signs: Cancer and Capricorn are tropical signs because the Sun is in these signs when it reaches the north and south solstices—the summer and winter solstices. The first degree of these signs marks the limits of the Sun's declination north and south of the Equator; the Tropic of Cancer, the Tropic of Capricorn.

Tropical Zodiac: This is the Zodiac initiated when the Sun enters Aries at the vernal equinox. It has nothing to do with the constellations of the Sidereal Zodiac. In fact, it has nothing to do with any constellations at all. It is merely the division of the 360 degree circle into 30 degree segments which are then given the names of the signs of the Zodiac, starting with Aries. This is the Zodiac astrologers use.

Truitine of Hermes: This is a very ancient system of rectification that requires a determination of the position of the Moon at the time of conception. My goodness! That is a chore that is easier said than done! How can one ever know the time of conception? It is a calculation that can never be proved.

Types: Type refers to a kind, class, or group having distinguishing characteristics in common. A type is an example, a model, an archetype. The signs of the Zodiac, if nothing else, do describe types; types of individuals, psychological types, types of behavior. And they are archetypes—original patterns of what they describe. We can never encounter a perfect example of one of these 12 archetypes because no one is ever born with all planets in one sign and that sign rising. Everybody is a collage of the 12 fundamental types which the signs describe.

Umbra: Umbra means "shadow," the total part of a shadow from within which the source of light cannot be seen at all. If the light source is a point, the whole shadow is umbra. If the light source has width, the umbra is surrounded by a penumbra.

Unaspected Planets: Occasionally in a horoscope there will be found a planet to which no major aspect is made by any of the other planets in the chart. This is a tremendous emphasis of the principle that the planet represents, and indicates that that planet operates with great purity through the medium of the sign it is in, unmodified as it is by contact with other planets.

Unfortunate Signs: No such animal. All of the signs represent an absolutely precious and essential mode of functioning, essential for wholeness and essential for survival. Our year would not be complete with one or another of the signs missing. The 12 signs are like the 12 old men in the forest in the old fairy tale: the wicked stepmother sent the poor maiden out into a winter storm to bring back strawberries. The girl came across the old men in the woods. Because she was polite and gentle, each of them blessed her with a special gift and the strawberries to boot!

Every sign has a positive and negative mode of manifestation. The determination of whether a sign will manifest in a positive or negative form probably depends on the soul within each individual, and not on some "star-crossed" configuration. Many people were born on the same day, and perhaps even at the same time, as Hitler.

Universal Time: A single agreed upon time for dating all astronomical events; it is equal to the local time at Greenwich, England on the zero meridian of longitude.

Uranian System: A system of astrological analysis devised by Witte, a ballistics officer in the German Army in World War I. He derived his method by applying astrology to events on the battlefield (which accounts for some of his more graphic descriptions of the significance of certain configurations — "burning bodies flying through the air" for instance). He believed that he found certain aspects more significant than others, and introduced the 90 degree dial to make these aspects more immediately visible. The 90 degree dial is simply a chart in which the four quarters of the circle are combined; thus all multiples of 90 degree aspects will appear as conjunctions, and all odd multiples of 45 degree aspects appear as oppositions.

Witte also introduced a total of eight hypothetical planets, whatever they are. Hypothetical planets?? With orbits yet, and to some of which have he gave the Greek names of the Roman gods for which the actual planets are named: Zeus, Poseidon, and Hades, for instance.

URANUS: Uranus was the first of the modern planets to be discovered, on March 13, 1781, by the German Astronomer, William Herschel.

The planet Uranus takes 84 years to complete his orbit. This planet has the least deviation from the Ecliptic than any of the other members of our solar system—less than a degree. The Ecliptic is of course determined by the Earth's path around the Sun. The orbits of all the other planets are more or less inclined to that plane. Not so Uranus. Being on the Ecliptic means it has the potential for eclipse. Therefore, when Uranus is conjunct with the Sun, the Sun is eclipsing it, and when Uranus is opposite the Sun, the Earth is between them, as is the case with a lunar eclipse. I do not know what this means, but it does point to a special connection between Sun, Earth, and Uranus. It is a very cold place.

The strangest thing about this eccentric planet is his inclination on his axis. The rotational axis of Uranus instead of pointing north and south as it does on all of the other planets, points east and west. (Recently it was discovered that this is the case with tiny Pluto, too.) Therefore the Equator on Uranus circles the planet north and south. The planet also rotates in the reverse direction from all the other planets except Venus. (Sunrise is in the west on Venus; but on Uranus, sunrise is north or south of the Ecliptic, depending on where it is in its orbit.) Because Uranus spins on its side, it exposes one pole to the sunlight for 42 years while the other pole is in darkness, then reverses the exposure for the next 42 years of its orbit. With all these eccentricities we could say this is a very perverse planet.

Uranus has a ring system, too, but his rings are composed of extremely dark material, which, unlike those of Saturn, are not coated with ice. It is the iciness of Saturn's rings that makes them so glorious, for this gives them greater reflectivity.

Mythologically, Uranus is god of the starry heavens. His consort is Mother Earth. Uranus feared that one of his children would injure him, so though he fertilized Mother Earth repeatedly, (her womb was filled with all kinds of creations and monsters), he forbade that she should bear any of her progeny. In anguish, Mother Earth appealed to her unborn children, and the only one to respond was Saturn, who took his little golden sickle and the next time that Uranus approached Mother Earth, Saturn castrated him. (The myth tells that when Uranus was castrated, the phallus fell into the sea "and surrounded by seafoam and mist, love and desire attached themselves to it and *Venus* was formed." In that age, the Aries Age, the masculine principle gained ascendancy. The feminine was degraded. And curiously, for all the macho hero stuff, homosexuality was rampant. Homosexuality is the eroticization of the masculine. Well, I wonder if this myth doesn't in some measure record those developments. I have noticed, by the way, that Aquarians often suffer from a vague undercurrent of castration anxiety. I have also noticed that physical beauty in the partner or sweetheart seems to be inordinately important to people with Aquarius rising. This sounds really dreadful, but mythological images are just like dreams, symbolic language, and I believe that this story is simply telling us that limits (Saturn) must be set on the unbounded creativity of the human mind. The scientific mind can be quite mad.

Uranus can be the archetype of a Frankenstein; the nutty professor, the detached scientist performing inhuman experiments. Realistic limits must be set on some "far-out" ideas and monstrous creations. Uranus rules Aquarius, an Introverted Thinking sign—the kind of thinking that the scientist and the ideologue do, a kind of thinking which can at times be very callous and detached. Consider the atomic bomb, star wars weapons, poison gas, doomsday machines, and some of "the end justifies the means" ideas of radical right or left political groups. (Of course, with regard to some of these scientific developments, other planets are involved, but the cool intellectual detachment required for scientific pursuit comes from Uranus and the sign he rules, Aquarius.) Another implication of the Saturn involvement is this: Saturn gives form to things. His castration of Uranus could be interpreted as saying "enough of your theories and abstract speculations; let's see the actual consequences of your creative urges. Let Mother Earth give birth."

Uranus is the principle of individuality, independence, nonconformity, and freedom. Aquarius, the sign he rules, is the sign of the brotherhood of man. There is a very high degree of social consciousness in this sign, and a tendency to idealize the perfect society. The opposite of Leo, (the divine right of kings) this sign is not at all egotistical or self-centered. There is a recognition in Aquarius of the unique individuality of all people and an unconstrained acceptance of the differences between individuals. Aquarius tends to be impersonal, casual, and easy-going. It is not at all a petty sign. Aquarians are often fun people who enjoy teasing and playing devil's advocate, often taking the opposite position in a discussion just for the sake of argument. There is often great loyalty to a person or a cause.

Uranus has much to do with all the sciences, especially astronomy, and with his discovery in 1781, the heavens really began to open up to us. The past two centuries have shown an incredible development in science.

In 1781, when Uranus was discovered, Ben Franklin was fooling around with his kite and key. Uranus certainly has to do with electricity, and by extension with "turning lights on," with bringing light, knowledge, or understanding in completely new and unexpected ways. Uranus is full of shocking surprises. Uranus exposes, he brings things to light. After all, he is god of the starry heavens, of the lights in the sky. With Uranus aspects there are often problems with electricity, such as blackouts and shortages, or surges of electrical energy. Uranus has to have an influence on the many electronics industries that exist today.

Uranus also releases energy. That is partly why he has much to do with earthquakes. Earthquakes occur when Mother Earth shifts her weight and releases energy. Therefore, without intending evil, Uranus is a destructive principle. But this is not necessarily negative. He destroys in order to make room for something new. Destruction should be followed by construction. But between the destruction and construction there can be considerable anxiety and pain: the rug has been pulled out from under one's feet, and there is no safe place to stand.

Uranus is the planet of revolution, and was discovered in the timely proximity of the American and French Revolutions. Uranus is always the indicator of revolutionary developments, for with Uranus, the status quo cannot be taken for granted. Often there are reversals in expectation, turnabouts, and changes in direction.

Uranian aspects are further geared to the future, focused on things to come, avant grade, progressive.

Negatively, Uranians can be weird, strange, alien, detached, and perverse. Uranus can be the indicator of shocking, and deviant behavior. This is the stuff of which nervous breakdowns are made. There may be revolutionary change and at the same time a fear of freedom, which then generate anxiety and alienation. Uranians are often ideologues who adamantly cling to an idea or ideal upon which they have pinned their hopes and dreams, stubbornly remaining loyal when change is required.

There is a mistaken attribution of inventiveness to this principle. Actually, invention is in the province of the asteroid Pallas, and when she joins up with Uranus, then high-tech invention is possible, inventions which make use of electricity and electronics or of the other sciences, for the world of science is in the sphere of Uranus.

VENUS: We see this gorgeous object as a morning or evening star, for she like Mercury can never get very far from the Sun. When she is visible, there is nothing brighter in the heavens, not even Jupiter. The cause of this brilliance is her dense carbon dioxide atmosphere, her cloud cover that reflects the light of the Sun. If it is true that atmosphere clouds perception, such folk sayings as "love is blind," "beauty is in the eye of the beholder," and even "beauty is only skin deep," may have their basis in fact. For under that heavy cloud cover, below her luminous veils, the surface of Venus is a broiling inferno—800 degrees Farenheit and more.

But the dense atmosphere on Venus has even greater significance. It creates what is called the "greenhouse effect." Solar energy, penetrating the cloud cover, is trapped on the surface of Venus, and there it remains and accumulates. It cannot escape into space as with other planets, such as our beautiful Earth, whose atmosphere is not so overwhelming that heat cannot be released. Venus hoards solar energy, she cannot let it go.

On Earth, the process of collecting and storing solar energy is called photosynthesis. We see it in the greening of the earth every spring, especially in May, Venus' month. The dictionary says that photosynthesis "is the production of organic substances, *chiefly sugars* from carbon dioxide and water occurring in green plant cells supplied with enough light to allow chlorophyll to aid in the transformation of the radiant energy into a chemical form." The green of our grasslands and forests is stored solar energy; it is the source of all life on Earth and very precious.

At one time (and still today in many cultures), cattle indicated wealth. Cows could be used for food and barter, but they were a cumbersome form of cash, and nowadays it is no longer necessary to display herds of animals or livestock to demonstrate wealth. We have invented a more convenient device to indicate value: money—which may take the form of coin or paper currency—greenbacks, as we call it in the U.S. Gold is a wonderful substance to represent solar energy or value, for it is a pure substance and is the color of the Sun itself—it is a perfect standard for wealth. Solar energy, that which Venus accumulates and which is stored in the plant life on earth and eaten by the grazing animals, is gold, greenbacks, money. Money symbolically represents potential energy—value, and is under the rulership of the planet Venus, for she is a collector; a storer of solar energy; a bank of solar energy. Venus rules banks. The bull, the zodiac animal of Taurus-Venus, is a creature of great potential energy. Traders in the stock market are called "Bulls." The stock market was founded in May.

Sugar is potential energy, and it is *chiefly sugars* that are produced through photosynthesis. Venus rules sugar, sweet stuff. The metal of Venus is copper, an excellent conductor of energy—heat.

These physical attributes of the planet Venus perfectly symbolize her astrological meaning as the indicator of potential energy, stored energy, contained energy, and therefore value. To put it simply, we might say that Venus has to do with those things which have value or worth, such as beauty and art, and with those things that symbolize value and worth, such as money and possessions.

But the planet Venus has other physical attributes. She is the only planet whose day is longer than her year. Venus makes one complete rotation on her axis every 243 days, and it takes 225 days for Venus to make one orbit around the Sun. She has a very leisurely day, as one astronomer put it. What's more, since Venus rotates in the opposite direction of all the planets but Uranus, sunrise on Venus is in the west. These facts, too, have symbolic meaning. I think they contribute to the Venusian caricature of inactivity and laziness, and as the indicator of endings, consummations, bringing things to completion. West for us symbolizes ending, and east beginning. We like things to end sweetly; we like happy endings to stories and sweet desserts at the end of meals. We like reward at the end of effort.

Also connected with the leisurely day of Venus and the tendency to accumulate energy is the passive-receptive nature of Venusian aspects. Inactivity. She is the opposite of Mars, remember. Activity burns or consumes energy, inactivity conserves it. Negatively, this manifests as laziness, negligence, indolence. She does not spend or release her energy; she hoards it, she is acquisitive.

Venus also has the most perfectly circular orbit of all the planets.

Mythologically, Venus is the goddess of pleasure. She was a beauty, the better to attract and ensnare. The only duty incumbent on Venus was to make love. She is the principle of completion, consummation, of gratification, of love, of pleasure. And although one may fall in love with Venus aspects, it is just as likely that a relationship will end. Sometimes one quits one's job, or gets fired, or retires. Venus is reward, rest after effort, payment after work. Venus is inactivity or the end of action.

She is the indicator of that which we value: beauty, art, pleasure, love, and that which means value itself; money. Venus is love because to love means to value, to appreciate. "Appreciate" is a Venusian word.

Sometimes the question of value can be very abstract. Value and worth can be applied to an idea, a social ideal, a utopian goal, which often happens when Venus is in Aquarius. Much depends on the sign she is in. She certainly is most materialistic in earth signs.

In the body, Venus and the sign she rules, Taurus, have to do with the throat and with anabolism, that aspect of metabolism which concerns the build-up of energy potential. It is interesting that the thyroid, which regulates the body's metabolism, is located in the throat. There are often health problems associated with sugar: diabetes, low blood-sugar, etc.

The Foundation for the Study of Cycles in Ervine, California says that there is a definite eight-year cycle with regard to money matters. And I have observed that Venus, with unremitting regularity, will have a station in the same sign every eight years. But not in every sign. Venus will have 20 stations in Virgo in this century, but only one in Libra.

Vertex: (see Antivertex)

Vertical: Directly overhead. The prime vertical is that circle in which a person stands upright facing south. It is sometimes called the circle of observation.

Vespertine: A planet setting just after the Sun has set is called "vespertine." A planet rising just before the Sun is called "matutine."

VESTA: The third largest asteroid, and the brightest. They say she is the only one of the four that can be seen with binoculars on a clear night at an appropriate time of the year. Perhaps this is because her orbital period is the shortest—a little more than three and one half years—which means she is closer to the Sun and Earth than any of the others. Her rotation period is five hours 20 minutes and she is inclined to the ecliptic about seven degrees. Ceres and Vesta, both of whom have the least eccentric orbits, seem to have the closest affinity with Virgo.

Mythologically, Vesta is the goddess of the hearth and the home. She is goddess of buildings as homes. Home is one's place of shelter, safety, and protection. It is where the family is, those with whom one belongs. The word "vesta" means hearth, and that word evokes images of warmth, coziness, food, and family gatherings. Vesta is the indicator of the family in a personal sense and in larger scope the nation, the state, and ethnic identity.

She is a very conservative principle, tending to support the status quo. Why shouldn't she? She is a very privileged goddess, the most secure of all. She always gets the first portion of any gift or sacrifice made to any of the gods. Small wonder that she doesn't want change, that she wants to preserve, to maintain, to keep all of the old customs intact. Also in the old ways and customs there is familiarity, tradition, and ongoingness, all of which contribute to the sense of safety, security, and belonging. The etymological root *vest* in many words provides clues to the meaning of Vesta. The vest itself is an article of clothing that provides warmth. We *invest* in the interest of security. Those who study the stock market and fail to consider Vesta have got themselves a lost cause. We in*vest*igate to determine the trustworthiness or credibility of information. When we are *vest*ed in our jobs we are assured of our pensions and our future security upon retirement. The term "*vest*ed interest" describes a close involvement with others to promote personal advantage, usually at the expense of others (the family protecting its own).

So it should not surprise us to find that a negative form of Vesta is the Mafia, the family that sells security. Another is any clan or group which puts its interests above all others, such as some secret societies and nationalist groups (the KKK, the Nazis).

Vesta is also connected to the protective services of the country—the police, the army and navy—and in*vest*igative agencies like the CIA, the FBI, and the NSA. Vesta is always active in cases of spying, including clandestine activities and industrial spying.

Vesta has to do with locks and keys, safes, security boxes

in banks, and the objects and devices we use to keep possessions safe. Vesta has to do with all kinds of safety precautions to protect against accident or fire. Vesta is the fire alarm and the burglar alarm. She alerts us to danger, as in the myth that tells us of the donkey's braying that awoke her as she dozed at a rustic festival and found the god Priapus about to mount her. She sent him scurrying, for Vesta is a virgin. The chastity belt is certainly a Vesta device. This was to insure fidelity to one's lord and master when patriarchy prevailed.

Purity is a Vesta concern that can be troublesome. Vesta takes pleasure in ethnic identity but she can worry too much about such things as racial and ethnic purity. She often suffers from xenophobia.

In her concern for safety and security she is the generator of vigilante groups, neighborhood guardians, and watchdogs, which may escalate into gangs who take the law into their own hands; lynch mobs.

Vesta is all kinds of insurance, as precaution for the future and in the event of disaster. Vesta is licensing, the legal indication that we have attained a certain degree of expertise which gives us the right to drive a car, to teach, to be real estate agents, to operate a business, etc.

With regard to spiritual matters, Vesta is the priesthood, those who have chosen to dedicate themselves to spiritual service. Many do wonderful work. But there are some who are extremely intolerant, one of Vesta's negative manifestations.

Vesta is a very important principle. There is no other planet that has to do with matters of safety, security, credibility, and trust.

Via Combusta: "The Burning Way." This is an archaic term for the stars in the constellation Scorpio, especially the first 15 degrees of that sign. In horary astrology, one of the "considerations before judgment" is that the Moon should not be located in the last 15 degrees of Libra nor in the first 15 degrees of Scorpio. This area of the Zodiac was thought to be fraught with danger. More medieval nonsense. It has a nice, dramatic, titillating ring to it, though: Via Combusta.

Violent Signs: Those signs that are the exaltations of Mars, Pluto, and Saturn, the so-called malefic planets; Aries, Scorpio, and Capricorn. Others assign this term to those signs that represent violent creatures. For your entertainment but not for your serious consideration.

VIRGO: Virgo is the third sign of the summer season. This is when the leaves begin to change color. The growing season is coming to an end, and harvest time is approaching with lots of work for the farmer. The dual aspect of this sign is that although this is a summer sign, and there may be days that are extremely hot, there also are days when the air is crisp, clear, and rather nippy, and we are thrown straight into fall. A day or two later summer reasserts itself and we go swimming to cool off.

This is an Earth sign, so it is primarily sensation, but because it is Mutable, or dual, another element is involved in its expression: thinking. Virgo manifests the psychological function, centroverted sensation-thinking, or thinking in relation to things. This is a very fussy sign. The expression "a place for everything and everything in its place" expresses the desire for ordering things, for sorting out, cataloging, tidying, for applying thought to matter. That is a necessity in this sign. For if these people don't try to keep order, they can get bogged down in so much detail that they may never extricate themselves. This is not to say that Virgo is always fussy and tidy and can never be a slob. Virgo can be a terrible slob. But usually there is some area of a Virgo's life that is or has to be in perfect order. Perhaps it is in work. Virgo may be a good statistician, doctor, nurse, health care worker, farmer, shopkeeper, computer programmer, or could be involved in any number of service occupations. For another important thing about this sign is they like to be of service and to share in work with others. These are people-persons too. Often they are very attracted to the helping professions; health and healing.

Ceres is the main ruler of this sign, and of course Ceres is a laboring productive principle, so people with Virgo rising or the Sun, Moon, or an unusual concentration of planets in this sign are not only hard workers (often they are workaholics), but are usually very productive as well as very caring. Their own tastes in food are inclined to be very simple, pure, and a surprising number of vegetarians are found here. Their own health problems may center around their digestive systems, especially the small intestine. Often they are colicky babies.

Virgo may be very critical at times, but usually in the interest of helping. Only your best friend will tell you certain things, and Virgo is that best friend. These people often have a sly, wry, caustic kind of wit. And for all the concern with purity that may be found here, no one can be so downright vulgar as Virgo.

Void of Course: In recent years a great fuss has been made of this nonexistent condition. It means that the Moon, having reached a certain degree of the sign through which she is moving, will no longer form a major aspect to any planet before she leaves that sign. For instance, if the Moon is in the 25th degree of a sign and there are no planets above the 25th degree in any sign, the Moon will have no planet to aspect until she enters the next sign and begins the journey from zero to 30 again. Only major aspects may be considered and all comets and asteroids are ignored.

The suggested implications of this "void of course" Moon are that errors in judgment will occur, plans for social and commercial enterprises will go haywire, and old or faulty mechanical equipment will tend to fail. On the other hand, it is believed that great insights are possible when the Moon is void of course (However, I don't see how that fits with the "errors in judgment" claim).

This is one of the "considerations before judgment" in horary astrology, which is a divinatory use of the principles of astrology and in that case may be acceptable. But in mundane astrology and in personal birth charts, I believe it is entirely inappropriate, for it is most unlikely that any degree of the Zodiac is unoccupied by either a planet, an asteroid or a comet. If aspects to asteroids and comets are effective in natal and mundane astrology, it makes no sense to leave them out here. If they were included it would be very unlikely that there would be a "void of course" Moon.

WATER SIGNS: The Water Triplicity contains the signs Cancer, Scorpio, and Pisces. One Cardinal, one Fixed, and one Mutable. They represent three aspects of the psychological function Intuition, which is to say they describe experience and perception by way of psychic means, by a kind of knowing without knowing how one knows. They "listen with the third ear," they see through surface appearances, they sense the potentials and possibilities of things. They are often prophetic, attuned to the future. Businessmen or women with planets in water, especially Cancer, are often leaders, way ahead of their colleagues in knowing what it is to which the public will be responsive. They are aware of coming trends but often so far ahead that they do not capitalize on it. They are in touch with things for which the world is very often not ready.

The water signs are feminine, and it is certainly of the water signs that people speak when they talk of "feminine intuition." Accompanying the intuitive perceptions of these water people, there is often a high degree of emotion.

Because of the emotional factor, these signs are often mistakenly called "feeling signs". Most people do not realize that there is a vast difference between feeling and emotion. Feeling is attitude inclination, judgement. "I love that color. I prefer it to this. This color is too noisy." Those are feeling judgments. There is nothing emotional about them. But if you say, "That color makes me feel sad" *that* is an emotional reaction behind which are hidden associations, memories, perhaps fears. "I feel really excited about this trip to Paris." That is definitely an expression of enthusiasm. But if you say, "I feel funny about this flight. Let's take a later plane", you are having an intuition probably accompanied by some foreboding emotions, that that flight may not be safe. You may be wrong, but it is a hunch and you would probably be wise to act on it.

Do you see the difference? Feelings are attitudes things. They are more direct, more positive, more willed, even when they are critical or harsh. Emotions are the reactions or responses to things. They are responses that happen to you, that simply present themselves, about which you are not required to make a conscious judgment and over which you have no control. Extreme emotional responses, of course, are tears and laughter, terror and panic, ecstasy.

In its extreme form, Water is the stuff of seers, psychics, mystics. In personality, certain water people will be found to be gullible, malleable, solicitous, compassionate. They respond and react to the influences around them. When J.B. Rhine was conducting his ESP experiments, found that when an emotional factor was present the ESP test scores were higher. Emotion seems to be a component of intuitive perception.

Water people will be found in many creative areas—painters, artists, dancers, musicians and in certain sciences, such as chemistry, in the oil industry, in plastics. They are great in business, imaginative, often poetic, good in advertising. They love the water, the seas, and many are attracted to maritime professions. They like to live near water.

They are often very empathetic and compassionate. They are not the most practical of people, often vague and unrealistic, but because they are not earthbound, their imaginations can soar, and they may come back from their flights of fancy with needed information about things to come.

Weak Signs: This is a medieval charge made against the signs Cancer and Pisces, with Capricorn thrown in for good measure. Well, if emotional responsiveness, empathy, compassion, readiness of tears, intuition, mediumship, spiritual consciousness, and self-giving are considered weak, then so be it. But as a matter of fact there is no sign more tenacious than Cancer as long as a positive potential exists, and Pisces often operates from such a powerful conviction of knowing that nothing can sway it. I find them to be exceedingly strong signs. Why Capricorn, an earthy, practical, realistic, no-nonsense kind of sign, is included with these two weepers I do not know.

WEATHER: The kind of weather prevalent at different times of the year in a general sense is shown by the signs; in other words, the seasons. You are more likely to find spring showers in March and April and snowfall and cold when the Sun and other planets are moving through the winter signs of Capricorn and Aquarius.

Neptune, Pluto, and the Moon—especially New and Full

Moons—and the water signs are associated with fogginess, mistiness, poor visibility, rain, and in extreme cases, torrential downpour and flooding.

Mars, Jupiter, and the Sun, especially in the Fire Signs, show hot, dry, arid conditions, or weather that is conducive to fire.

Juno, Pallas, sometimes Mercury, Uranus, and the Air Signs are associated with windy weather.

Venus, Ceres, Vesta, Saturn, and the Earth Signs are indicators of dryness. Yes, including Saturn, for the wintry phenomenon of this planet and the sign it rules, Capricorn, is snow or water crystallized, given form: water that does not flow.

But interesting things happen weatherwise when these four elements and the planets that rule them combine with each other in various ways:

Fire and Earth: Fiery signs and planets in combination with earthy planets and signs are suggestive of drought and desert-like, arid conditions.

Wind and Earth: windy or airy signs and planets in combination with Earth signs and planets are more likely to produce tornadoes; wind on land.

Wind and Water: Airy planets and signs in combination with watery planets and signs are more likely to show hurricane or typhoon; wind over water or wet winds.

Fire and Water: Fiery signs and planets involved with watery planets and signs certainly can generate steamy hot and humid conditions, tropical storms, summer storms.

Fire and Air: Obviously the right combination for hot air.

216

Like the Santa Ana winds; hot and moist if water is also involved.

But one of the most important recent developments in astrology with regard to weather is the recognition of the importance of the asteroid Juno as an indicator of weather or atmosphere. Juno is an atmospheric principle (the winds obey her) and the atmosphere, environment, and the quality of life are in her sphere. And there is no doubt about it, weather is the prime measure of the quality of life.

An example of the way in which Juno operates: In *Planet Watch* there is a calendar section in which, a month ahead of time, I describe the mutual aspects between the planets, and try to envisage the potential manifestation of these planetary combinations. The entry for September 17th 1989 was; "Juno square Jupiter in 8 Libra-Cancer 11. Much turbulence. Windy. Hurricane or tornado likely in places with receptors. Turbulent. Hectic." That was the day Hurricane Hugo battered Jamaica. A few days later on September 21st I recorded, "Juno square Neptune in 9 Libra-Capricorn 37 . . . . . this can also be indicating storminess, torrential rain, hurricane. . . ." This was when the hurricane had reached the coast of southern states and began to wreak its havoc there. These comments were written the full month before, in August.

Notice that Water and Air signs were involved in the first instance, with the stormy goddess Juno in the turbulent Air Sign Libra and the planet of bigness and excess in the Water Sign Cancer. In the second instance, Juno was still in turbulent Air but the Water planet Neptune was in the Earth Sign, Capricorn. Wind and Water, Wind and Earth.

217

Yod: (see Configurations)
Young Moon: When the moon has just passed its New Moon position and is becoming visible to the east of the Sun.

Zenith: The point in the heavens immediately overhead. The Midheaven planets close to this point are said to be more powerful. I don't know. The point directly overhead is somewhere around the ninth and tenth houses. Planets in this area of the chart are simply doing the work that is required of them with regard to the circumstances indicated by those two houses.

ZODIAC: The Circle of Animals. This is the imaginary belt in the heavens extending about eight degrees on either side of the Ecliptic, the apparent path of the Sun on its yearly journey. The constellations found in this belt have been given the names of animals for the most part; the Ram, the Bull, the Lion, the Goat. These are the constellations of the Zodiac. Actually, it is the path of the Earth's journey in its orbit around the Sun which we transfer to the Sun. It is in this vicinity, this band of the heavens, this plane, where most of the other planets and the Moon also orbit the Sun. Only those bodies whose orbits are extremely inclined to the Ecliptic ever move out of this band of constellations. But remember that these constellations of the Zodiac are not the same as the signs of the Zodiac. Because of precession, the constellations are offset relative to the signs, and when the Sun enters the *sign* Aries, the actual *constellation* behind the Sun is still Pisces. The Zodiac consists of the following animal and human allegorical representatives:

Aries the Ram. It is in the springtime that lambs are born. Adult rams sport gorgeous horns with which they batter each other heads for the privilege of mating with as many ewes as possible. Perhaps the ram symbolizes the aggressiveness of the creative urge that is a characteristic of those born with the Sun in Aries, Aries rising or with an unusual concentration of planets in this sign.

Taurus the Bull. Like the sheep and the goat, the bull is a grazer, but his great strength, contained power, and potential energy make him a more fitting creature to represent Taurus, the month of the greening of the Earth, when, through the process of photosynthesis, the earth captures and stores solar energy creating the forage upon which the bull depends for life. The bull a was symbol for wealth in earlier cultures, and remains so even today; in stock market lingo a "bull market" is one of high confidence and abundance.

Gemini the Twins. Siblings. It is said that children learn more quickly when there are other siblings around. Having brothers and sisters near one's own age means that there is always someone with whom to communicate, with whom to share perceptions and feelings. Conducive to more social functioning.

Cancer the Crab. Symbolic of the sideways and often indirect approach to things that certain natives of this sign exhibit. The Crab is most unwilling to let go of what it has until something else is well in hand; it symbolizes the stamina of the sign Cancer. For all its emotionality, and often ready tears, there is great strength and tenacity in Cancer, which, like the crab, holds on while brutal tidal currents tug and pull at it. It know its time will come, that the tide will change.

Leo the Lion. Every inch a king. That is a regal animal, confident, sandy colored, gorgeously maned, occasionally letting out a threatening growl or roar when intruders approach, but mostly content to laze in the shade and doze in the midst of his pride, until informed that one of his lionesses has made a kill and it's dinner time. He has few challengers of his own species, and none of any other.

Virgo the Virgin holding the Sheaf of Wheat. She is Ceres, the goddess of the harvest, whose own emblem is the Horn of Plenty. Virgo is a farmer. Perhaps the sheaf of wheat, or corn or barley she holds aside from indicating food, and therefore survival also represents the multitude of details that must be attended to and kept in order in any labor or work if one is to be productive and feed one's family. She labors to produce. Giving birth is called labor.

Libra with the Scales of Justice. This symbolizes judgment, weighing the evidence, seeing how one thing balances against another. The Libran glyph of the scales reminds us how important justice is to all relationships. If there is injustice there must be recourse to law. For those who lack power, justice under the law is the only refuge. Pallas Athena, goddess of wisdom and justice, and Juno, goddess of marrage, childbirth, and the powerless, know what this means: using thought, reason, and understanding to avoid conflict and make reasonable adjustment of differences. And if that doesn't work take it to court.

Scorpio the Scorpion. The scorpion is another crustacean. But the main characteristic of this creature is its deadly sting which they say it will use against itself if push comes to shove, and there is no other way out. The scorpion will survive, triumph . . . or else. But, like the Phoenix, another Scorpio creature, it will rise again out of its ashes. I really think the Phoenix is a more appropriate, less surly representative of this exceedingly creative sign.

Sagittarius the Centaur. When Sagittarius arrives it is the time of the hunter—fall. The horse symbolizes the physical, animal aspect of Sagittarius and the upper human body and head the idea of mind over matter. The arrow he shoots represents transcendence. Through travel, learning, raising our consciousness we may aspire to transcend our baser instincts without deserting them altogether. We may learn how to unite, to make as one our animal and human natures.

Capricorn the Goat. Another grazer, but this one lives on the Mountain, in Capricorn country. This is an old-young, young-old sign. The bearded goat has to survive a much harsher habitat than the bull and ram—rocky, hilly terrain—and dig for his forage through winter snows. A sure-footed, lusty creature. But Capricorn is also the frolicsome kid prancing on the mountainside.

Aquarius the Water Bearer. Like the other two Air signs Libra and Gemini and Virgo, which, being Mutable, partakes of Air to some degree, Aquarius is represented by a human

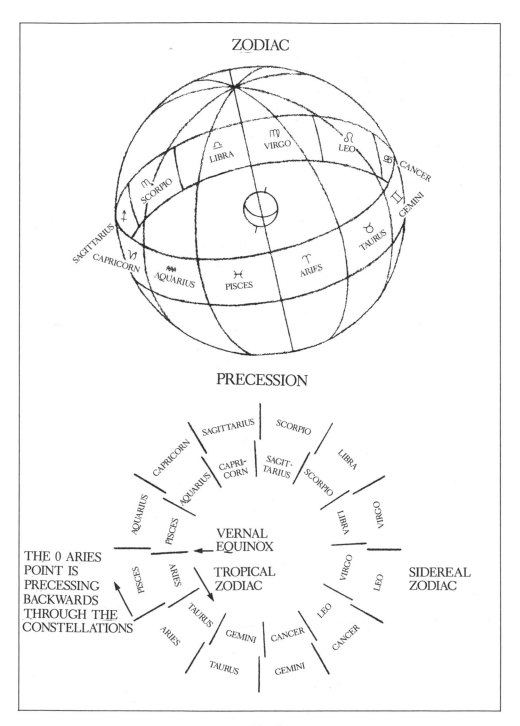

ZODIAC

PRECESSION

VERNAL
EQUINOX

TROPICAL
ZODIAC

SIDEREAL
ZODIAC

THE 0 ARIES
POINT IS
PRECESSING
BACKWARDS
THROUGH THE
CONSTELLATIONS

figure. He holds two urns from which he pours fertilizing waters on the Earth below. This corresponds to the Tarot card called *The Star,* an image of a young, nude female with one foot in a stream and the other on land. From two urns she pours water on the Earth and in the stream. The waters represent knowledge, wisdom, and understanding. Aquarius does have a Water sign, Pisces, on one side and an Earth sign, Capricorn, on the other.

Pisces the Fish. That which abounds in the great maternal watery realm from whence we have all emerged. Denizens of the sea ride and yield to the currents, streams, and tides and wear the uniform of their fellows. Egolessness and oneness with God are more important then individual separateness and isolation. You are not alone in Pisces; you are a part of everything and everything is a part of you.

(It is interesting that people born with a particular emphasis in a sign often feel a great affinity for their totem animals. For instance I am Capricorn and I love goats. It turns out that when I was an infant, my mother's milk ran dry. Fortunately in the small town in Pennsylvania where I was born, there lived an old Italian man named "Old Falconi," who kept a nanny goat. Every day he brought my mother the nanny's milk for her new baby. I was raised on goat's milk for the first year or two of my life.) (see Precession)